# BORDERS MATTER

Homeland Security and the Search for North America

Daniel Drache

Fernwood Publishing • Halifax, Nova Scotia

Editing: Douglas Beall
Cover image: Richard Slye
Design and production: Beverley Rach
Printed and bound in Canada by: Hignell Printing Limited

A publication of:
Fernwood Publishing
Site 2A, Box 5, 8422 St. Margaret's Bay Road
Black Point, Nova Scotia, B0J 1B0
and 324 Clare Avenue
Winnipeg, Manitoba, R3L 1S3
www.fernwoodbooks.ca

Fernwood Publishing Company Limited gratefully acknowledges
the financial support of the Department of Canadian Heritage,
the Nova Scotia Department of Tourism and Culture
and the Canada Council for the Arts for our publishing program.

National Library of Canada Cataloguing in Publication

Drache, Daniel, 1941-
Borders matter: Homeland Security and the search for North
America / Daniel Drache.

Includes bibliographical references.
ISBN 1-55266-123-7

1. Boundaries—Social aspects—Canada. 2. Canada—Boundaries—United States. 3. United States—Boundaries—Canada. I. Title.

FC180.D73 2004     971     C2003-906818-8

# CONTENTS

This book is dedicated to my father, who taught me much about the staying power of the Great Border

"There is no worse flaw in man's character
than that of wanting to belong."
—David Adams Richards, from *Mercy Among the Children*

"Perhaps people in the world are kinder everywhere than
maps of the words would lead you to believe."
—William Boyd, from *Any Human Heart*

# PREFACE

## Permeable Borders

Until September 11, 2001, Canadians had not thought very much or very hard about the long border they share with the US. Nor had public authorities shown significant concern. There was no compelling imperative to contemplate it, particularly in this global age. Ideas passed through it, money poured over it and millions of people crossed it each year. Post–September 11, the border has changed beyond recognition. It is everywhere and everything. Issues now include enhanced security, protection of privacy rights, who we want as citizens, how cross-border traffic can be expedited and how open the border should be to political refugees.

In fact, the world's longest undefended border was never unimportant. It has always been at centre stage in North America in the exercise of power and international cooperation.

Arguably, Canadians and Americans have come to understand each other less and less, and there are profound differences in how they think about the Great Border. The North American Free Trade Agreement (NAFTA) downsized the importance of national boundaries and minimized their importance as regulatory gates and commercial walls. Now Canada finds itself in a new relationship with the US. There is precious little to negotiate, as Washington expects Canada to get with the program, no questions asked. The security wall is forbidding and many of the old notions about a porous border no longer apply. The security needs of the US now reach into our domestic space and the effects are pronounced.

## New Rules of the Game

Washington's Homeland Security Act has redefined and reconfigured the border in a way that is neither anti- or pro-border, but is totally different from what anyone had predicted when NAFTA was signed a decade ago. Canadians are security outsiders as far as US law is concerned, and it is the intent of the US Congress to regard Canada as no different than any other foreign power. We are now "imprisoned" in North America. Supposedly we must choose between the border as an identity line in the sand for citizenship purposes and our strategic self-interest.

## The Challenge of Our Borders

Canadians have not often been nimble or successful in defining, let alone defending, their strategic self-interests. We have always walked a perilously thin line between our competing national-isms, regionalisms and localisms, and the blunt reality of being a smallish dependent economy vulnerable to US pressures. We don't relish being offside. Our elites prefer onside agreements, such as free trade, negotiated in Washington and Geneva. However, we now have little alternative but to learn the science of skilled positioning domestically and internationally.

The challenge of our borders as a strategic policy issue requires getting the fundamentals straight. If we are to come to terms with our new status on the continent in this divisive age and to defend our national self-interest, it is important to realize that Canada is part of a new North American paradigm from which no region is exempt. To maintain maximum manoeuvrability, we need to know what our assets are, no less than our liabilities. It may be, as Denis Stairs argues, that Canada has receded into a very modest place in world affairs as its dependency on the US has grown.[1] Yet another reality is that the emphasis on US homeland security has done more to revive Canadian nationalism than any other force since the 1960s.

This book asks these basic questions about the Great Border. Why does the border pose such a dilemma to Canadians (Chapter 1)? However artificial a border is between two countries, why has the Canada-US border been so resistant to globalization pressures to dismantle it (Chapter 2)? What accounts for so much divergence in social standards and regional cultures (Chapter 3)? Is the North American community heading towards an era of broadening and deepening (Chapter 4)? How must Canada address the unilateralism of US homeland security (Chapter 5)? Finally, how has the security-first border transformed Canadian sovereignty (Chapter 6)?

Stephen Clarkson began his encyclopedic and prescient volume *Uncle Sam and Us* by describing how, when NAFTA became law, he wore a mental black arm band signifying the death of Canada. A decade later, though, Canada is more politically robust and independent-minded than before. For example, we said no to sending troops to Iraq and, unlike the US, ratified the Kyoto Protocol. Canada signalled a desire to legalize marijuana and gay marriages. Even in this age of unprecedented integration, Canada's welfare state displays a remarkable tenacity to survive financial cutbacks, public carelessness, policy stupidity, collective neglect, media hostility and broken promises. The contrast with the US welfare state, dismantled in 1996 by President Bill Clinton, is stark. Canada's was shrunk but not torn down, and its largest programs consume almost half of the federal budget.

## The Blind Spot of Morbidity Politics

Many on the Left believe that the Canadian welfare state has shrunk to the size of a hobbit. The Right thinks it is wrestling with an 800-pound gorilla. "Social Canada," to use a phrase in fashion today, is neither hobbit nor gorilla. Canada's social policy regime is more comprehensive, universal and redistributive than its US counterpart by a long stretch. Three of Canada's top social policy analysts conclude that "the distribution of disposable income was more equal in 1997 than in 1974."[2] Any story of the border must assess the economic rationality of this institution. Its regulatory impacts affect who we are as citizens with rights and responsibilities for one another.

Not surprisingly there is a large political constituency which does not want Canada to compromise its principles or the welfare state in order to maximize relations with the US, as a *Globe and Mail* readers poll revealed on June 2, 2003. Out of close to fifteen thousand respondents,76 percent said no to jeopardizing Canadian sovereignty for more access to the US market. The results shocked many business elites who believe that public opinion is supposed to follow the market imperative towards more integration. Instead, the public's resolve to shape reality rather than being overtaken by it has stiffened. Certainly today, Canadians from all regions have less faith in American leadership than at any time in recent history. Moral conservatism is at the margins of Canadian political life. The steady decline of the Alliance Party, the closest thing Canadians have to the US Republican Party, from a high of over 25 percent scarcely three years earlier to about 10 percent in 2003 polls speaks volumes. Canadians are worried about the future of continental integration, and discerning Canadians want to increase their sovereignty, not compromise it any further.

Quebecers don't have the same hang-ups about politics as fate. They don't write books about the end of Quebec, or the death of *la belle province* in North America. Federalists have long wished that the sovereignists would throw up their hands in despair about the asymmetry of power between Quebec and the rest of Canada, but Quebec nationalists never have. Although their part of Canada is small, not as wealthy as Ontario and one of the most dependent of any Canadian region on the US as a market for its exports, modern Quebecers have learned to think outside the box of economic determinism and to strike a more realistic balance between their economic and political agendas.

Canada's corporate elites are way out of step with mainstream Canadian public opinion. They have recurrent anxiety attacks about their place in North America and want their fellow citizens to believe that Canada's almost unlimited access to the US market is in peril. But where is the convincing evidence for this allegation? They want to get rid of the border, seeing it as an impediment to cross-border integration. How ill-informed they are! Since 9/11, no US official has ever proposed that Ford or IBM Canada stop exporting goods to their American head offices. To listen to corporate Canada's main public message, you would think that the Great Border separating the two countries is almost shut down to cross-border traffic. Nonsense.

The facts are that in recent years, on a per capita basis, Canadians have purchased almost $6,000 of US goods while Americans bought only $375 of Canadian products. The flows have never come close to balancing. For the last thirty years, US exports to Canada have remain fixed at about three percent of its GDP. The two free-trade agreements have hardly put a dint in the number. By contrast, Canadian exports to the US soared to more than 37 percent of GDP in 2001.[3] For day tripping, cheap eats, family outings, and bargain-based shopping visits to Niagara Falls, Fort Erie, Lewiston, Pembina, Gateway or Blaine, the border flows are largely unmanaged. For everything else, there are all kinds of large and small effects that need to be examined, analyzed and understood.

## The Tipping Point

For instance, free trade has punched big holes in the Canada-US border, leaving it highly porous to goods and services, and to the select category of people able to acquire professional visas to move across the border to corporate headquarters in the US. Only a tiny number of Canadians and Americans have relocated permanently. Market fundamentalism has affected all of us in other ways. The very prospect of an incipient North American community exudes the idea of dynamic progress. Building the North American community is one of those "big" ideas that needs to be addressed in real time. Does it have a future, a soft present or only a dim past? This too is an important-looking hypothesis that needs clear and finely-honed analysis.

The great North American border has always been a blend of the "porous" and the "impermeable." It is like a giant connector plug, to borrow from Thomas Friedman[4]; when this plug misfires or isn't working as it should, it creates a bad connection between Canada and the US. Canadians feel the effects of this distortion. If the border in all of its aspects is working well, then Canadian sovereignty as applied statecraft will be effective and focused. But, whether through neglect or indifference, if we don't have the fundamentals down pat, then all the rhetoric about "joined at the hip by geography and the head by mentality" won't make a bit of difference.

Distance and perspective are required to free ourselves from many of the old debates about economic integration. We are at a "tipping point" where an array of forces are pushing and pulling Canada-US relations towards a new configuration with different rules, practices, ideas and mentalities.

To look at North America with this understanding will help us identify the processes and behaviours that will change outcomes globally and locally. To identify a tipping point, or points, is a strategic way to map and track the complex issues put in play at a time of fluidity and great moment. A good beginning is to recognize the singular importance of the border to who we are and to the political economy of Canada. It is time to consider our future in this way. Even though we are more trapped in North America, we are also separate and apart.[5] We are not irreversibly driven towards one model of social and political life in North America.[6]

Why? Dani Rodrik's powerful answer in *Has Globalization Gone Too Far?* is that open economies need social protection. Canada is a classic test case of this hypothesis. We spend four percent more of our GDP on income security than our neighbour; we value citizenship more than national identity; we have a stronger social bond and believe in the value of most things public in ways strikingly different from the republic to the south. The debate on whether national differences in North America are more important than similarities has not produced a definitive answer, nor could it. If spending reflects priorities and values, Canadians and Americans are increasingly on the way to becoming very different societies. At one time we were look-alikes in many areas, but now our distinctiveness is unquestionable. Nonetheless, Canadians must get their act together and focus on the essential, and that is the need for public authority to exercise its power and work on our behalf at the border as well as behind and beyond it.

## Friends at a Distance: The New Dynamic

If there is a single message in this book, it is that being a prudent, middle-power country with a perennial lack of confidence should not be confused with being voiceless or powerless. When we Canadians obsess about our "sparse demography and vast geography," we do poorly in managing the border, the most important measure of our relationship with the US. But when the concentration is on our separate but parallel destinies, and on finding ways to reduce the asymmetry of power, Canadian public policy can be creative and move away from traditional reflexes. The northern federation need not be confined by narrowly economistic policy prescriptions driven by "irreversible" US market pressures.

Across the continent, disruptive cultural and economic changes are forcing governments, businesses and civil society to look at all the options for re-imagining national communities and their interdependence. At present, values and institutions on both sides of the border matter more than ever. With so much divergence in views the two countries are not copies of each other. A new dynamic is present. The US deficit is spiralling out of control while the Canadian deficit has been wrestled to the ground, leaving Ottawa with an important surplus to spend on rebuilding the social bond. With Quebec sovereignty and the national unity question pushed to the back burner, Canada-US relations may well become the number one priority for the Martin government. This is the story that is about to be told. We have to get closer to ourselves and to understand our relationship with the US as, in Henry David Thoreau's words, "friends at a distance." We ought not to have shirked our responsibility to get a handle on the complex issue of the border, and now we have no alternative but to put things right.

# 1. BORDERS PERMEABLE AND IMPERMEABLE: CANADA'S IMMEDIATE DILEMMA

> "Canada is essentially closer to the United States than it is to itself." —Paul Krugman, from *Geography and Trade*

## The Clash of Sovereignties

Borders are always tense places where bureaucracy, red tape and the minutiae of rules are menacing and inescapable. When you are entering the US at one of the dozens of border crossings that separate the two countries, if you are not a citizen of that country, you don't know what your rights are or whether you have any at all. One moment you are Canadian, but by crossing that official line you acquire the status of tourist, immigrant or alien. On your return, you take a deep breath and are glad to be home. Perhaps you are cosmopolitan with other identities and loyalties that transcend your nationality, but in that brief moment of return a surge of feeling is telling you, the sojourner, that you belong and are protected by a state that is not theirs but your own.

Suppose you are an anti-nationalist and reject the nation-state as your primary civic standard. Is it really any different? Your twelve-page passport cannot account for the sense of belonging that involuntarily stirs the emotions. You are part of a political community with rights, obligations and a belief in a common structure of experiences. Here is the very beginning of the modern notion of citizenship, which is "created out of social realities," as Isin reminds us.[1] For no society are borders a modern anachronism. Borders protect a country's institutions, the behaviour of its people and the experiences of all kinds of groups in comparison to those of their neighbours. A border bisects markets, affecting investment and production decisions, and is one of society's most powerful institutional markers, functioning as a regulatory wall, commercial gate, security moat and line in the sand for citizenship purposes.

North America's Great Border has always presented an intractable dilemma. Contrary to the national myth that good fences make for good neighbours, joint management of the forty-ninth parallel has never been insurance that the peaceable kingdom of this vast continent has been well shared when vital US interests are in play. Some one hundred and fifty cross-border agreements govern the border, and there is formal cooperation between Canadian and American security, customs, police, transportation, environmental, tax and agricultural officials.

Much of the governance function is also conducted through informal contacts and ad hoc arrangements between US departments and Canadian ministries. High and low bureaucrats email each other, consult on the phone and meet at conferences. Seen in this light, the Canada-US border cannot be regarded as a second-order, one-dimensional institution from another age. Rather, it represents the real and symbolic battle line where two sovereignties have quarrelled and skirmished to advance their strategic interests. The great Republic and the northern Confederation have clashed most over their common undefended border about resources, access to markets, security needs, cultural visions, entry procedures, citizenship rules and the criteria for political refugee status.

Post–September 11 we are still sorting out the effects of all the legislative changes to border rules and practices for immigration and security, and to the framework for North American defence (see Figure 1). So far there is no policy model, social theory or policy yardstick that grasps the complex, multidimensional and dramatic changes to North America's borders in their roles as security moat, commercial gate, regulatory fence and identity line for citizenship.

This is worrisome for Canadians who have yet to redefine their national interests post-9/11. Americans have no such hesitation. They have been expanding their security state since 1947, when, on July 26, Congress passed the National Security Act quietly and without much national debate. This Act created legislative machinery and independent intelligence agencies, largely unaccountable to Congress, to defend US national interests

*Figure 1. The Canada/United States Border Pre-9/11*

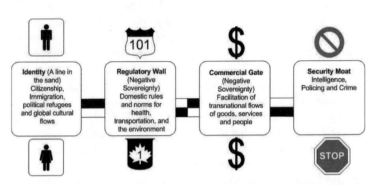

against foreign power threats.[2] A great deal of American interest continues to be defined by the logic, if not the mindset, of the National Security Act. US foreign policy has long been value-driven; mixing up the unflinching pursuit of national interests with what Condoleezza Rice, President George W. Bush's National Security Advisor, labels "second-order effects" that "benefit all humanity." America's moral mission now puts Canadians directly in the line of fire of the new US security doctrine, which calls for pre-emptive action against rogue states and their terrorist clients, and assumes that allies are loyalists, not sceptics.

The result is that the undefended border has been transformed into a heavily policed and militarized frontier. Current Canada-US border politics are going to be intense and unlike any in the previous century. In a security-obsessed world, the politics of the Canadian border require smart, independent thinking and nerves of steel. The important questions to ask are: How are Ottawa and Canadians planning to address these dramatically changed circumstances? Are we in charge of our side of the border any longer? Can we be? What policies and models of the border are best suited to our needs?

## A Second Hinge Moment

Post–September 11 the undefended, people-friendly, open border has disappeared forever. From Washington's perspective there is no longer a shared Canada-US consensus that each country is responsible for its own side of the fence. The establishment of the US Department of Homeland Security represents the largest governmental reorganization in the last fifty years. It has a \$40-billion budget, employs 150,000 personnel and is now in charge of all aspects of US security domestically, continentally and globally.[3] It is the lead actor inside government, singly mandated to coordinate the framework of homeland defence with the Executive, House of Representatives, Senate, and the US judiciary, intelligence agencies and the military chiefs of staff.

The mandate of this monster-sized department applies to all aspects of US security at, behind and beyond the border. The Department of Homeland Security acts with administrative, political and legal authority to take any measures and actions deemed necessary, globally or locally, to protect US interests. It is the arms, legs and nerve centre of Washington's national security doctrine, coordinating, directing and overseeing US security needs. It reaches down into the local community and links every municipality and city to Washington. Responsibility for the border is shared by the departments of State and Transportation, the International Boundary Commission, the Environmental Protection Agency, the General Services Administration, Customs, Immigration and Naturalization, the Department of Agriculture and state, county and local authorities. Almost every sizeable governmental department has a piece of the action. Homeland security is now part of the fabric of American society and government and will outlast the Bush presidency. It is a permanent institutional change that Congress will not alter for a long time to come. Border effects on markets, already large, will soon become larger and the impact on Canada will be even greater because so many agendas are in play.

Some agendas are security-driven and demanding, others are intelligence-focused and require covert and overt surveillance in the US and far beyond its borders, still others that appear to be highly technical are politically motivated—immigration, for example. Cumulatively the impacts are huge for all countries. Congress has used the Homeland Security Act to take control of its side of the fence and a good part of Canada's side as well.

Many Canadians do not understand the extent to which US law and institutional arrangements have changed. Nor are Canadians particularly gifted readers of US presidential intent and the multi-centred, diffuse nature of US politics. We are still operating on our old assumptions and belief in the power of good neighbourliness. Our business elites continue to believe, in Bruce Hutchinson's classic words, that the border is "a perpetual diplomatic dialogue … a fact of nature … which no man thinks of changing."[4] But certainly it is no longer that.

The essential character of the new rules is that they are mandated by US law and operate through the executive arm of government, with little opportunity for public review and active input. Foreign input is nil or after the fact. Any talks or discussions that occur with Canada, Mexico or other countries are within American terms of reference and backed by the full power of US law. The orbit of the new security act seems to be limitless. Everything is considered to be "in the interests of our safety" according to the US State Department.[5] It is completely open-ended and can be used equally for foreign retribution or domestic persecution. Statements such as, "for the good of our wider security," put the global community on notice that the power and interests of the US extend everywhere. As the cornerstone legislation of Bush's imperial presidency, the Homeland Security Act is nothing less than a constitutional revolution. It gives the Executive extraordinary power to take pre-emptive action abroad, and at home it removes the democratic restraints on the Justice Department that prevented it from conducting surveillance of any kind without probable cause or court sanction.

US Homeland Security has already begun implementing vast changes to US security practices in all areas. It

- establishes demanding regulations for visitors, political refugees and immigrants to the US,
- creates new security requirements for travellers, exporters, land, sea and air carriers, vehicles and companies on all aspects of security that affect US national interests,
- transforms the role of police and intelligence for operations in a global, continental, regional and local environment as a seamless organization for national security,
- coordinates intelligence gathering across government and establishes new standards and operating codes that authorize

electronic surveillance on individuals and groups without writ or permission of a higher court judge,

- authorizes practices and procedures that effectively reduce the privacy rights of individuals and allow the security authority to collect information that can be turned over to police and judicial agencies with few civil rights safeguards,
- requires foreign visitors to the US to submit to new procedures including fingerprinting and other kinds of security checks that will be entered into the computers and records of the US security system, and
- upgrades the US security infrastructure and its capacity to respond to new terrorist threats in the future. [6]

All of these security goals directly concern Canada and the future of the forty-ninth parallel. For instance, transborder transportation is being rethought with respect to vehicle inspections, security checks on drivers and other issues.

With minimal consultation and no negotiation, Canada and Mexico were informed that the entire continental transportation system—the heart of the continental economy—had been re-regulated. The magnitude of this so-called "technical change" is reminiscent of an equally dramatic moment in 1939 when US authorities unilaterally demanded that all Canadians entering the US have passports.

Canada signed the Smart Border Accord in December 2001, an action plan, in the language of the US security doctrine, "to ensure the secure flow of goods, people, infrastructure and information sharing." The aim was to facilitate pre-clearance in both countries. The Accord builds on NEXUS and CANPASS, two programs negotiated between Ottawa and Washington that require Canadian truckers to meet "rigorous security standards" set by US security personnel. Border security pre-clearance raises fundamental issues about the balance between security and privacy.[7] These bilateral programs subject Canadians to the authority of both the Patriot and Homeland Security Acts in ways that are unprecedented.

Other aspects of the homeland security strategy have consequences for Canada's energy development, transportation policies and international cooperation. In the near future, it is conceivable that, armed with the authority of the homeland security doctrine, Washington could decide that the security of its water supply requires Canada to negotiate a water-sharing agreement. The Paley Report looked at US energy needs through this prism.[8] Energy is essential to security, and discussions on a formal, continental sharing agreement are well advanced.

The implications of US security needs are still being worked out in other areas by the Bush administration, and this must be closely monitored by Ottawa. So far, though, there is no top-level Canadian governmental structure mandated to produce a major audit of all the US statutes that bear directly or indirectly on Canada. No public legal assessment of the impact of homeland security on Canada's Charter of Rights and Freedoms has been released to clarify the potential or actual violations this US law poses with respect to the rights of Canadian immigrants and political refugees. Nor has there been any fundamental examination of the impact of US security needs with respect to NAFTA provisions and US trade law generally. Canada's parliament has not debated the extralegal dimension of homeland security and its effects on cross-border management.

It is a mistake to think that since most of the changes in the new security legislation are directed at US citizens, and not Canadians, that Canada should not be unduly concerned. The 2001 Patriot Act, formally named, "Uniting and Strengthening America by Providing Appropriate Tools Required to Intercept and Obstruct Terrorism," gives sweeping powers to border and other police agencies on an unprecedented scale.[9] For instance, it authorizes secret hearings, denies detainees access to legal representation and provides new powers for search and surveillance that are "largely outside of the purview of the legislature and the judiciary."[10] The Centre for Constitutional Rights, a Washington-based think tank, has documented how the new legislation has weakened the checks and balances of the US system, and the extent to which the courts are now deferring to the Executive. It legalizes the kind of furtive spying that Lyndon Johnson employed on anti-war groups and Richard Nixon authorized in the Watergate break-ins. This unparalleled increase in executive power at the expense of other branches of government is without precedent in the history of modern US presidents and undermines the constitutional rights of citizens and non-citizens alike.

These invasive security practices apply no less vigorously to the management of the Canada-US border. For instance, much of the legislation is set by executive order and interim agency regulations without prior public comment or congressional input. The rules are not fixed in stone but depend on what the Executive decides is necessary and fitting. It gives the president and Congress maximum flexibility to respond ad hoc and arbitrarily if it is in American interests to do so. Under law, US customs and border officials have acquired wide discretionary powers with respect to immigrants, visas and visitors. Since 9/11 the legal strictures have become tighter, more selective and more rule-driven. Immigration officers used to be proud that theirs was a service-driven department; now it is 100 percent security-oriented.[11]

Some administrative and legal changes have already been announced, and all are invasive, demanding and non-negotiable for Canada and other countries. The Bush administration's new rules and regulations around food security exports are typical and reflect how dramatic the impact of the security-first border will be for some producers. In response to the possible dangers of a bioterrorist attack on US food imports, the US Congress has imposed new rules and regulations.[12] Canadian exporters will have to pre-alert US authorities to all shipments to US customers, pre-inspection of food products will be mandatory and new paperwork is required with obligatory full disclosure of all ingredients and their source countries. Canadian exporters will have to pay new service charges to have their shipments cleared by US Customs. For these producers, the border is no longer seamless, but if they want to export to the US, they will have to comply. Canadian exporters are worried about the bureaucratic red tape and the increases to their costs. If it is no longer worth their while to continue exporting to the US, they may have to find other markets.

## Goods and People Face a Different Future

Other changes are equally pronounced and far-reaching. Canadian landed immigrants from more than fifty countries now require visas to visit the US, and these can be obtained only with a security clearance. This latest change affects hundreds of thousands of landed immigrants from Canada's large Indian and South Asian communities. A Canadian landed immigrant who wants to visit family or take a vacation is required to submit to a security check by US officials. Even if refused entry, they are not entitled to know the criteria used to arrive at this decision. The border is closing for them, and many will face restrictive and arbitrary treatment should they choose to travel to the US.

Foreign-born Canadian citizens travelling in the US have even been deported to their country of birth. Maher Arar, a Canadian citizen born in Syria, was arrested in 2002 in New York while travelling home to Ottawa. Despite his Canadian citizenship, US authorities deported him to Syria without notifying Canadian authorities, and there he remained in jail for more than a year without being formally charged.[13]

The EU has said a loud no to the invasion of privacy rights. At least it has put up a fight for the time being. Why has Ottawa not had the same courage to defend all Canadian citizens under the Charter of Rights and Freedoms? Article 6 gives every citizen, whether born here or not, the right to enter, leave and remain in Canada. At the border there should be no difference between native-born Canadians and those who have chosen Canada as their new home.[14] Ottawa is on the firing line to protect landed immigrants from this discriminatory and arbitrary treatment, but so far there is no strategy or policy in place to protect landed immigrants from US authorities.

Ottawa has largely cooperated with the Bush administration in the areas of immigration and security, typecasting the immigrant as a potential or real threat. In record haste, Canada's national government passed Bill C-11, The Immigration and Refugee Protection Act, in November 2002. It expands the government's detention powers over immigrants who are deemed "security risks" and reduces the mechanism for independent review of ministerial security decisions, allowing the detention of individuals on a security certificate indefinitely without appeal. Bill C-36, The Anti-Terrorism Act, gives Ottawa and police agencies new powers to deport, detain and prosecute citizens and non-citizens under police suspicion because of their ethnic background or association with immigrant communities.[15]

Whereas NAFTA opened the border, US homeland security regulations have re-tightened it to an unparalleled degree. For goods, the gate is still open, but for newcomers to North America, it operates as a skintight filter. Fewer immigrants and many fewer refugees will get through the new complex procedures and security checks. Further, immigrants who have been denied status in the US will no longer be accepted in Canada as they had been previously, because Ottawa and Washington have signed an agreement to end this practice. Particularly disturbing is Article 6 of the Canada-US Safe Third County Agreement, which broadens the unilateral powers of the US and Canada to examine any immigrant's status claim "when it determines that it is in its public interest to do so."[16] Members of ethno-cultural minorities are going to be singled out under the new agreement. US law provides for expedited removal of immigrants that authorities deem a threat to US security. This powerful weapon gives American authorities a wide arc of discretionary power.

In August 2003, using these new powers, Immigration Canada detained twenty-one Pakistani students on security certificates. No charges were laid, because under Canada's recently passed security laws, the process is secretive and charges are not required. Although they were 470 other cases of irregularities with student visas, none of these were detained or investigated. Racial profiling seemed to be the primary factor in the twenty-one arrests. In a public statement in September 2003, the RCMP said they regarded none of the Pakistani students as a security risk, but only a handful were released. The others remained in detention without being formally charged. [17]

Under the new rules, goods and people face very different futures. Canadian elites are worried that US authorities will close the border and disrupt just-in-time production chains, but it is a fiction to believe that the border is about to close to goods. Waiting lines for trucks crossing the border have almost returned to normal. On average, waits are less than an hour, pretty much what they were before 9/11.

There will be delays and periodic border slowdowns whenever US authorities decide to increase inspections, but it is in the interests of the US to ensure that just-in-time production chains operate efficiently. The head of Chrysler Canada has publicly stated that his company has experienced no major problems in shipping or receiving goods. Corporate America has voiced no public complaints about the transborder flow of goods between the two integrated economies.[18] US production has not been unduly disrupted for any length of time. The ebb and flow of the cross-border traffic in goods does not capture the essential truth that the US and Canada are on fundamentally different paths, and that Ottawa has yet to face the problem head on.

## Unilateralism and the Security-First Border

Homeland security is a bare-knuckle, unilateral policy framework that is not rules-based and negotiated like NAFTA. There is no hint of partnership somewhere down the road, nor is the idea of political integration contemplated. Homeland security is based on American self-interest and the unilateral exercise of power. The US does not ask if its allies or even its closest neighbour approves of boarding the "security" train. They are expected to be on it. From the American perspective, the US will rely on its own military and legislative framework to secure its interests both globally and continentally. It will cooperate with other countries when it suits American interests to do so, but just as frequently it will act unilaterally. Bush put it starkly, "When it comes to our security, we really don't need anybody's permission."[19] The homeland security doctrine is the embodiment of undivided sovereignty— the US sets down the rules for others.

All of this points to a fundamental paradigm shift for Canadians. Canadian sovereignty will be more contested because the homeland security doctrine is proactive, aggressively single-minded, consciously comprehensive and largely self-reliant. At the centre of the new order looms the security needs of a border that is no longer strictly defined by territory but primarily by self-interest. Neither Washington nor Ottawa can avoid the bounded nature of the border. When American elites join the dots together, they see only one Great Border in North America, most of it American by design and now by US law. The longest undefended defence perimeter in the world is manned and policed by its armed forces and border guards.

The Protective Moat or Canada's Civic Identity?

Canadians need to reflect long and hard about the border as a moat for security and as a boundary marker for identity and citizenship. Canadians are not good jugglers of these conflicting agendas. We do not, as second nature, think in terms of strategic self-interest. Rather, Canadian governments have followed a strategy of indirection and compliance, minimizing the strategic effects of the border in the hope of currying favour with Washington. Ottawa has rarely behaved as a powerful nation might in using defence of its border policies for nationalistic ends. Instead, Canadian governments have always treated border politics first and foremost as a pragmatic issue, as a means to provide access to the US market, as a regulatory screen to uphold public interest standards and as a low-maintenance security perimeter. The border was never a lightning rod for national territorial ambition, largely because the great undefended border was settled in 1846 by the Oregon Treaty and has not moved a centimetre since. Canada and the US have quarrelled in modern times about the exact position of the border in the Strait of Juan de Fuca and George's Strait, and over Arctic sovereignty, but no Canadian or American is ready to go to war to defend the integrity of their side of the border.[20]

As far back as the Treaty of Versailles, which redrew the map of the modern world in 1919, Canada has gravitated to the role of quiet diplomat, brokering policy differences between the US and Britain.[21] Sir Robert Borden, Canada's prime minister in 1919, was the self-appointed liaison between Lloyd George and Woodrow Wilson. Unlike Britain, France and India in the modern period, Canada has no history of defending its own vital interests globally, or of holding sharply opposing views to Washington on global politics.

Trudeau's third option was an attempt to give Canada an independent voice on the global stage befitting a regional power, but his experiment collapsed. Our exports to all of Latin America amount to less than one percent of Canada's total. Even our trade with the EU is minuscule given the size of its market and our social and cultural ties with its members. Since 1989, merchandise trade with G-7 countries decreased as Canada became more dependent on the US. By 1998 the UK took merely 1.7 percent of Canada's exports, Germany 1.4 percent, France 1.1 percent and Italy only 0.8 percent.[22] Japan is our second largest trading partner but comprises less than 4 percent of our total trade. No Canadian government has been able to convince the business elite that access to other markets would give Canada new leverage in Washington.

Prior to the US war in Iraq, Canada was rarely to be found in the ranks of the dissenters. John Diefenbaker, Canada's populist (and wrongly cast as anti-American) prime minister, killed the Avro Arrow, the leading Canadian jet fighter of the 1950s, and bought US warplanes instead, ending any hope of a modern Canadian aviation industry. Lester Pearson accepted Bomarc missiles, and later prime ministers pushed for close diplomatic, military and economic ties with the Republic. In defence and military matters, Canada specialized in niche security operations. The prototypical bilateral institution was NORAD, established in 1958 for the defence of North America, largely paid for by Washington and operated by US personnel. Lacking a large military capacity, Canada's elite diplomatic core regularly made small but symbolic contributions to North American defence in multilateral settings. Ottawa cast its lot with the US during the Cold War, was good at UN peacekeeping and received kudos as a middle power for its high profile, behind-the-scenes work at the UN and in front-line peacekeeping.[23]

## The Good Neighbour Syndrome: Weakness or Strength?

The good neighbour syndrome warrants some critical examination. Canadians like to cling to the myth that friendship buys influence within the world's most powerful state. The reality is that few US presidents have taken strategic advice on how they should exercise power from their commercial neighbour. One of the most public attempts at advice-giving occurred during the 1960s when Prime Minister Pearson criticized the US bombing of Vietnam. Although Canadians applauded Pearson's principled stand, he was terrified by President Johnson's wrath, according to historians. Pearson wasn't punished for being off-side and, despite his stance, his government succeeded in negotiating the Auto Pact, the one measure that arguably did more to transform the industrial structure of Canada than any other. But Johnson did not button his lip either. He rebuked Pearson in public and abused him verbally in private at Camp David. "You pissed on my rug," LBJ shouted while grabbing Pearson's lapels. Tensions between the neighbours rose, but in the end diplomacy prevailed. The relationship between the two countries remained strong and unbroken despite Canada's criticism of US bombing.

Post–September 11, the politics of the border require a great deal of smart, independent thinking and action about applied sovereignty, and the setting of national priorities. Americans have redefined their national interests concerning security, trade and homeland defence. More immediately, the US has groped to find a rationale for the war in Iraq, since the raison d'être for pre-emptive action was undermined by the failure to discover weapons of mass destruction. The US government is at odds with its principal allies and with many Americans. It is unable to see the world through the eyes of weaker powers and is blinded by the strength of its own mythology and the dominance of its own culture.[24] "America first–ism" has naturally produced a very different assessment of threats and the proper means to deal with them.

The disparity in power between the Republic and the Confederation has opened a large ideological gap with regard to the role of law and international institutions. In the past, Canadian officials thought they knew how to maintain an effective relationship with the US, but now they are not sure. The Bush Doctrine calls for the pursuit of American dominance through pre-emptive military action. It also commits the US to further policy initiatives of deterrence and containment. Cooperative action and renewed commitment to multilateralism and international legal norms are far down on its list. In the current, security-dominated universe, should Canada continue to try to be the insider or is there another path through which we might make a constructive international contribution?

So far, Canada's business elites have displayed no capacity to reverse course and think outside the traditional commerce-at-any-price box. They have failed to recognize that, domestically, there is broad political support for George Washington's wise counsel that "There can be no greater error than to expect or calculate upon real favour from nation to nation."[25]

## Imperial Right and Wrong: A World without Favour

Carrying on without "favour" requires that Canada redefine its objectives and chart its own course. It needs to distance itself, as much as possible, from the entangling web of US unilateralism. We can do this by degrees and also by kind. Our goal is, in the words of Denis Stairs, to "build up our foreign policy assets."[26] It is not that the policy step is so large, as Canada's decision to ratify the Kyoto Protocol, when the US did not, testifies. The much greater hurdle is the shift in mentality and the de-identification with our "significant other."

As Washington increasingly operates from the idea of imperial right, the rules of the game will change constantly and abruptly. For middle powers, NAFTA-like mega agreements come with a high price attached: they lack adequate exit provisions. NAFTA does not protect Canada from US trade protectionism. So something different is required that does not institutionalize the disparity of power between the two countries. The operative idea of Andrew Cooper is "calculated ambivalence," not ambiguity.[27] Canada does not want to be high up on Washington's security-first radar screen. It needs distance and time to strategize and to listen to Canadian public opinion. Political positioning is first and foremost a strategic act. By necessity, Canadian diplomatic responses to US policy will be much more ad hoc and influenced by what other US allies are thinking and doing.

Canada wants to decide who its allies are on the merit of the case just like any other nation-state. This is much easier to effect now that the Atlantic Alliance is less functional and its politics more complex than at any previous time since World War II. In the new world order, Canadians are not convinced that their destiny is always to play the role of the acquiescent deputy sheriff in the "coalition of the willing." The question is: Can a "middle-power" country learn to manage its relationship with Washington when the economics of the commercial gate seem to be everything and strategic self-interest only a vague concept?

## Inside North America: Separate and Parallel

In their much-read volume, *Empire,* Hardt and Negri put their finger on Canada's immediate quandary: "Empire presents its order as permanent, eternal and necessary." Security is presented as having a strong ethical basis. In the world of empire, the guardians present every issue as essential and requiring unconditional support from its allies. The empire builds its new order so large and global that "it envelops the entire space of what it considers civilisation."[28] In reality, however, each country must make decisions based on a finely honed sense of its own national self-interest, which will determine its own security needs. This will involve other considerations such as cultural and political integrity, not to mention its own understanding of its international obligations.[29]

We Canadians need to probe the idea of our outsider status, and this will take much ingenuity, reflection and hard work. We must question it, refine it and give it legs and substance. As the US moves to precipitate more regime change globally, new responses are required from each of its allies. Robert Kagan, in his influential book, *Of Paradise and Power*, explains the psychology of power and American weakness from a realistic perspective:

> Strong powers naturally view the world differently than weaker powers. They measure risks and threats differently, they define security differently, and they have different levels of tolerance for insecurity. Those who have great military power are more likely to consider force a useful tool of international relations than those who have less military power.... American propensity to military action recalls the old saw "when you have a hammer, all problems look like nails."[30]

Geopolitical logic requires a different response from Canada.

The border has always been the political membrane through which people, wealth, goods and information must pass before they are considered acceptable to public authority. The basic rule of every border, even in this borderless age, is that all cars, trucks, boats, people and ships must be checked in and out. Borders thus remain indispensable to control transborder traffic and to protect public safety during health crises, such as SARS. The US closed the border to Canadian beef when a single case of mad cow disease was discovered in Alberta. Regulators from the US Food and Drug Administration responded very forcefully when California planned to import cheaper Canadian drugs. The assistant commissioner for policy said that any attempt to bring in Canadians drugs would be a violation of US law and "a compromise on safety."[31] Globalization may reduce the centrality of the border as a lever of public policy, but the state continues to need it for public safety, protection of the environment and most areas of public life.

Contrary to what many believe, borders are permanent revenue generators. In 1999, Canada's border generated \$22 billion in taxes, duties and fees.[32] Canadians even pay for their sovereignty when they buy goods on the Internet, because the state, acting as revenue police, collects GST and PST for every article that comes into Canada.

## Borders in a Free Trade Era

Had Ottawa systematically gathered knowledge on the border as a public policy issue, it might have observed that the border segments markets with respect to economic performance, social policy, trade patterns and domestic immigration to the US. The economic evidence points to an unorthodox conclusion: Although Canadians and Americans increasingly share one market, they do not live in a single economy subject to the same institutional pressures and outcomes.

The detailed and sophisticated empirical analyses of John Helliwell, Andrew Sharpe, Andrew Jackson, Gerard Boychuk, Michael Wolfson, Keith Banting, Richard Simeon, George Hoberg, Lars Osberg and John McCallum have revealed that both small and large differences persist and have not diminished despite pressures from the global marketplace to conform and adapt. Their findings flatly contradict the principal claim of the free trade model that identity and borders are not supposed to count for very much against the powerful integrative forces aligned to consolidate the continental economy.[33]

First McCallum, and later Helliwell, two of Canada's most innovative economists, compared interprovincial and international trade densities in order to measure the importance of distance in export markets and assess the degree to which globalization had reduced the relative importance of borders. To their amazement they found, using a gravity model to measure the impact of distance on exports, that Canadians ship nearly three times as much to other Canadians as they do to the US.[34] Even with all the trade resulting from the Canada-US Free Trade Agreement, Helliwell discovered that "interprovincial trade linkages are still twelve times tighter than those between states and provinces."[35]

Growth in exports does not reflect a borderless world. Far from it. If borders didn't matter, the findings of such studies would be reversed. Canadian exports should have risen, given the opportunity to do business with the 200 million Americans who live beyond the border states. On this key issue, Helliwell and McKitrick discovered that "international linkages remain less dense than those within the national economy." Canadian provinces, no less than US states, rely on their national and regional financial markets as much as ever. That markets are, in Helliwell's and McKitrick's words, "segmented by national boundaries" is a powerful notion.[36]

## Divergence and Not Straight-Line Convergence

From a policy perspective, Helliwell's findings point in a singular direction. The great North American border may be less important as a commercial gate, but it is still important as a regulatory and protective wall:

- Ottawa continues to be a primary agent for the redistribution of public goods. In 2000, Ottawa collected $38.6 billion more in revenue from the three wealthiest provinces—Ontario, British Columbia and Alberta—than it spent. This amounts to $2,020 per person.[37] In the seven other provinces, Ottawa spent almost $18 billion more than it collected in revenues, or $1,475 per person.
- Without Ottawa's redistributive hand, some provinces would need to double their tax rates in order to provide comparable services—Newfoundland's tax rate would double, while Quebec's tax rate would increase by about 5 percent and Saskatchewan's by 8 percent.[38]
- Public responsibility has devolved to states and provinces in North America to an unprecedented degree. In the past twenty-five years, Ottawa has gone from keeping 48 percent of all taxes raised to only 41 percent. The municipal share has

declined marginally from 10 percent to 9 percent. The greatest shift has come about as a result of decentralization. During this time, provincial governments have increased their share of the tax pie to 37 percent, up from 33 percent.[39] According to an OECD study, Washington holds back about 45 percent of all taxes raised, state governments 20 percent, and local governments 12 percent.[40] These percentages have not changed significantly since 1975, despite Washington's downloading of fiscal conservatism onto individual states.

Increasing integration has not narrowed the scope for distinctive programs and politics on the northern part of the continent. The two countries continue to evolve on separate pathways. Taxes and government transfers remain cornerstone policies in Canada. In the US, the absence of government transfers has polarized income differences between states. Canada and the US have remained socially and economically distinct.[42]

Globalization has been unable to generate a way of organizing political life outside the nation-state. We have no way of knowing who is a citizen and who is not without identifying a person's nationality. In a fundamental way, citizenship and borders have renationalized politics and community at a time of North American integration. Canadians are now border-conscious in a way no one could have predicted.

The ascendance of Paul Martin could easily reverse the ad hoc "*independentiste*" policies of the Chrétien government. He could seek a special place inside Bush's homeland security doctrine. He could agree to the new missile defence system now in the works. And he could endorse the establishment of a Northern Command that would place Canadian forces under the Pentagon.

The idea behind "interoperability" would give Canadians forces, in theory, access to the latest US weaponry, operations organization and military strategies, but this is the wrong policy choice. Canada's armed forces are already too US-centric and dependent on the US military establishment for status, prestige and the latest weaponry. In practice Canadian forces get professional training like the Chileans, Mexicans, Germans, British and Brazilians at prestigious US staff colleges. They don't get access to any US secrets, but Canadian officers who go for career advancement return to Canada predisposed to US military values and dependent on US military strategic thinking. In the process they have lost much of their capacity to think of what is best for Canada's strategic interests.

These long-standing arrangements for Canadian military integration into a US command and operations structure were the consequence of the Ogdensburg agreement signed between FDR and Mackenzie King in the early 1940s. This agreement and many others extolled the virtues of Canada-US cooperation. In recent decades the tradition of the Ogdensburg model appealed to the high command in Canada's armed forces, especially the notion that the two military commands had few significant differences in outlook. Canadian officers believed that they had the same goals, values and needs. Canada's top commanders believed that they could participate independently and with US forces for common ends. Today homeland security has rewritten the rules.

The "coalition of the willing" is under the direct control of the US military and Congress. There is no pretence that decision-making will be shared as it is in NATO, which operates on an alliance model of joint decision-making. Today the US has so much power that the equalitarian pretence of past arrangements is being dispensed with. It is not ready to share information or give up command and control to win over reluctant coalition partners. American military superiority is so overwhelming that Canada's capacity to plug in to this new military system is very limited. So what can be Canada's military role, faced with the American need for quick and nimble intervention worldwide?[43] Should we upgrade our UN peacekeeping capability and strengthen our military to be more effective in multilateral operations?

We need to answer the question of whether we have any place in the seamless US framework? This is the unprecedented challenge facing Canada's new prime minister. Homeland security is not an alliance where the cooperation of allies is needed. It is a different world where Canada and the US have differing assessments of the threats and the means for dealing with them and of the meaning of international law and institutions. With the US largely indifferent to the interdependence that defines the world of the twenty-first century, a large and highly visible strategic and ideological gap has opened between the two neighbours. The US does not look to its Canadian ally to be constrained, and neither does Canada have the means or influence to affect American power and behaviour on the world stage. An irreversible turning point in Canada-US relations has been reached.

## 2. A Stellar Decade for Borders: But Do They Matter Any Longer?

> "Crossing the border is like ripping the continent, tearing its invisible casing." —Clark Blaise, from *The Border as Fiction*

Crossing the Undefended Canada-US Border:
So Much Anxiety Still

Compared to others, the 1990s was a very good decade for national frontiers. According to Daniel Latouche, who has calculated the growth of borders, over forty new borders were created, or about 4.3 a year![1] Many new countries emerged on the world stage following the breakup of the communist bloc and the Balkans, not to mention de facto borders set up by the warring factions in the developing world. For example, East Germany saw its borders with Poland and Czechoslovakia disappear when the two Germanies were reunited and Germany acquired new borders.

Superficially our age shares little with the world of 1919, when the Paris Peace Treaty redrew the map of the world in six breathless months. The victorious allied powers parcelled out the once mighty Ottoman and Austro-Hungarian empires to themselves, Germany was dismembered and older nations such as Poland, Estonia and Latvia reappeared from the ruins of Tsarist Russia.[2] The number of borders keeps increasing and few countries disappeared from the face of the planet in the nineties.

In our time, it is mental borders that have shifted precipitously with the destructive forces of nationalism, religious fundamentalism and tribalism emerging after long absence. Older paradigms such as Marxism have almost disappeared from the world of state power and policy. Strikingly, boundaries remain as much rigidly ideational as they are territorial. Today, countries are signing treaties and international agreements and undertakings at a record rate. Currently more than 3,500 treaties of all kinds are said to exist between states. This is hardly evidence of the borderless world that many predicted would emerge with globalization. The unified "global village" of Marshall McLuhan's celebrated metaphor does not mesh with what is happening on the ground. The inequalities between the global rich and poor have erected new barriers. Countries with long-established frontiers are trying to patch up the "leaks," doing their best to reinvent their borders to reflect pressing sovereignty agendas such as limiting cross-border crime, reducing illegal immigration and granting political asylum.

## Patching the Leaks of Sovereignty

Between 2000 and 2003, over 300,000 illegal migrants were detained or expelled by US border authorities. In 2001 the single largest category of individuals detained or expelled were those who failed to present proper documents. In the same year, over 185,000 individuals were removed from US national territory— 71,000 for criminal offences and 113,000 for non-criminal offences.[3] Mexicans represent the largest category of those who were turned back or deported, according to US Immigration statistics.[4] A recent study by the US Congressional Office reveals that Canadians constitute the fourth largest group of illegal residents in the US.[5]

In the UK, Prime Minister Tony Blair expected that the number of asylum applications will be halved in 2004, as a result of the newly passed Asylum and Immigration Act. Blair projected that the number of asylum applications would drop from a high of 92,000 before September 11 to between 30,000 and 40,000. Britains are worried that this Act will result in the UK defaulting on its international obligations under the Convention of Human Rights and to the EU.[6]

The ability to control the movement of "citizens" through the issuance of passports helped transform the nation-state. Now familiar binaries such as friend-enemy and stranger-citizen, became the foundation of national politics. The introduction of the passport was a critical moment for consolidating internal and external sovereignty. However, travel documents existed long before the modern nation-state. In his history of modern Islam, Bernard Lewis observes that Muslim emissaries were regularly sent to the West and were furnished with diplomatic letters of introduction.[7] The modern passport, although a product of the French Revolution, was not widely adopted until the early part of the twentieth century. Before then, European countries had permeable borders with few border guards. John Keegan catches the permeability of the lazy frontier of prewar days in this memorable sentence: "[One] crossed without passports at the infrequent customs posts and without formality anywhere."[8] France abolished passports and visas in 1861. Other countries would follow suit, and prior to World War I, Europe had abolished this police document.

It is often forgotten that, prior to 1914, millions of people came to North America without visas and travel documents. Border controls were few and checkpoints minimal. Controls came in after the flood tide of immigration following the "dangerous foreigner" scare in the 1920s. Those who found themselves on boats to the US were checked in at Ellis Island and for the hundreds of thousands of immigrants who chose Canada, Halifax was the great port of disembarkment. The general result of this growth in immigration controls was that "local borders were replaced by national ones, and the chief difficulty associated with human movement was entry into, not departure from, territorial spaces."[9]

## Designing the Imperialist Border by Accidental Intent

The birth of the modern passport was but one instance of growing state control over individuals. In both peace and wartime, governments have understood the power of passports. In 1915 the Canadian government dropped the old practice of issuing travel documents signed by the Governor General. The first modern passport was issued in English only. In 1926 a series of conferences on international passports led to the first bilingual Canadian passport as French was still the lingua franca of diplomacy. In the 1930s, Canadians were directed to the Canadian legation instead of the British passport office. The largest single change came in 1939 when Washington unilaterally announced that Canadians would require passports, visas and other kinds of travel documents to cross the border. Until then about half a million Canadians had visited the US annually without formal documentation. Only belatedly, in 1947, did Canada begin issuing Canadian passports for Canadian citizens, the result of the passage of the National Citizenship Act. This was the first statute of substance that established domicile and naturalization through the immigration machinery of the state. It took eighty years after Confederation before Canadian citizenship with a distinct legal identity separate from Britain was finally promulgated.[10]

Today in North America the Great Border sometimes appears artificial and contrived to those who cross it daily. However, the imperative to control and organize national space started with the emergence of the nation-state in the eighteenth and nineteenth centuries. Once the surface of the earth could be mapped precisely and the bounds of land and sea measured with scientific mapping, the rush to establish geographical boundaries took on a life of its own.

Countries went to war over borders, seized the land of others and made peace by trading territories that did not belong to them, dividing and re-dividing the world with a passion rarely seen. European borders and national sovereignty were established by custom, balance of power, the modern peace treaty and, most of all, by sheer political will.[11] By the nineteenth century, with the New World divided up, European powers marched into Africa and Asia, carving up the world's remaining continents like real estate developers. Much like today's advocates of a borderless world, they seemed to think it possible to obliterate existing borders from civic memory.[12]

French, British and Italian explorers rushed to lay claim by outright occupation to "the huge expanse of empty space" in Africa. Alan Moorhead's classic history, *The White Nile*, captures the spirit of this rapacious age, describing how, after the fall of Khartoum in 1885, the French explorer Marchand marched across the continent and claimed the Sudan for France! It is hard to believe that France and England were prepared to go to war over distant Sudan. The British Foreign Office sent no less than General Kitchener, fresh from victory at Omdurman, to assert British rights over French. With France mobilizing "to fight for the Sudan," Marchand and Kitchener met aboard the British general's gunboat for a champagne lunch to settle the issue.[13] Somewhere between *le plat principal* and the dessert, they took out the map and drew a line that became the border of Sudan. The geopoliticians of the day cared little about human geography. The great powers treated non-Western continents as blank spaces to be mapped, delineated and occupied.

Geographers, geologists, soldiers of fortune, jurists, scientists, missionaries, explorers, dreamers, scoundrels, pamphleteers, millions of immigrants and the persecuted became part of this historical movement to impose frontiers on new lands as well as older, settled countries. Defining a border was no mean task, and many factors from artifice to greed were determinant. Nation-building, sovereignty and borders became inseparable parts of national identities. North America was no exception to this rule and often served as a standard of imperial conquest. The processes of drawing lines in the so-called New World were as arbitrary and accidental as anywhere else on the globe.

## North American Myth-Making and the Border

Historians have found it peculiar that the early borders of the North American continent were haphazardly determined by treaties that only mentioned lines of longitude. However, the earliest French documents relied on lines of latitude, being first used in 1603 when Champlain set Canada's eastern boundary as between 40 and 46 degrees latitude, an area that included the region between Cape Cod and Cape Breton. Proclamation of sovereignty in the New World was a crude affair, dependent upon great power rivalries rather than defined principles.[14]

The standard procedure was to extend political sovereignty from a settled area to an unknown one. Laying claim to vast unknown lands became the regular practice of French, British, Spanish and Dutch explorers. In 1761, Jeffreys maintained that Canada's limit in the west extended "over countries and nations hitherto undiscovered." In 1795, the Duc de la Rochefoucauld was bolder, claiming that Upper Canada was comprised of "all the known and unknown countries extending as far as the Pacific … and is bounded also northwards by unknown countries."[15]

The Artifice of the Great Map of North America:
Drawing Lines and Evoking the Imperial Interest

The word "countries" was deliberate and meant not to recognize aboriginal entitlement and existing political organizations. In the pre-European period, aboriginal peoples' demands for territorial boundaries arose from the need for food. Hunting territories, with boundaries determined by rivers, ridges, lakes and other natural landmarks, formed the accepted political and geographic boundary markers for the Algonkian tribes. Native peoples in southeastern Canada used watersheds as boundary markers. Nicholson tells us that in "what is now New Brunswick, Martins Head on the Bay of Fundy probably separated the Micmacs and Malecites, and Point Lepreau the Saint John River Indians from the Passamaquoddies."[16]

European colonizers and invaders believed North America was a tabula rasa upon which they could impose any design or boundary their minds could conceive of. When James I granted Nova Scotia to Sir William Alexander, the patent was all the more remarkable because so much was unknown about the territory and its borders. Ignorance of terrain was not a barrier to the European powers. The language of this patent is a vivid reminder of the way the continent was partitioned. It describes the territory as "stretching along the Sea, westward to the roadstead of St. Mary, commonly called St. Mary's Bay and thence northward by a straight line ... to the great roadstead Bay of Fundy." The reader then comes across a very strange phrase. The patent speaks of an imaginary straight line "conceived to extend through the land, or run northward to the nearest bay, river, or stream emptying into the great river of Canada."[17] Arbitrarily imposing an imaginary straight line on land that had not yet been explored to create a map few understood was first and foremost an exercise in politics.

Drawing "the map" was always an exercise in politics and conquest that the British and other imperial powers like France, Spain and Portugal quickly mastered. The map meant ownership in a world of geopolitical rivalry. For instance, in the official 1795 map of the Annapolis Valley and the Maritime region on view at the University of Mount Alison's art gallery in Sackville, New Brunswick, what is most striking is that all evidence of the earlier Acadian settlement had been erased, and this map was of course in English. The British cartographer had largely copied the earlier French cartographer's map, removing any French place names of the Acadians who had lived in the Annapolis Valley since the early 1700s. In 1755 the British had brutally expelled ten thousand Acadian settlers from the choice Annapolis Valley, where they had lived and farmed for decades, to make way for British immigrants. Many Acadians made their way to Louisiana, but others evaded the British and remained in the region illegally. The 1795 British map had just empty spaces waiting to be filled. It was as if the British had come to this region first; everything previously present had been consciously suppressed. In Benedict Andersen's words, maps created the real and imaginary empire for the settler, and no less for British public consumption. The map made ownership "real" and authoritatively legal.[18]

## Joining the Dots on the Map: The Divine Right of Kings

The view of the great North American historical geographer D.W. Meinig, in his three-volume *The Shaping of America,* was that the organization of interior North America did not correspond to actual modern state needs until the latter half of the eighteenth century. According to Meinig, the great turning point in creating the modern notion of North America was unquestionably the Proclamation Line of 1763. The Proclamation Line used geography on a continental scale to demarcate a boundary line that separated European settlers from indigenous peoples and reorganized the interior. Indian territories were recognized, Quebec's boundaries were delimited, Newfoundland's boundaries were adjusted, Nova Scotia's were demarcated with greater precision and the Crown was given vast lands, which it retains to this day.[19]

The success of the American Revolution forever changed the map of North America. With the signing of the Treaty of Paris in 1783, North America was reorganized into discrete national entities with a recognizable border that delineated two very distinct societies with different systems for justice, collection of taxes and customs, policing and religious affairs. Those who felt trapped by the new American state exited to Canada. Almost one hundred thousand Loyalists travelled north, and within less than a decade the border came to represent a natural geographic point of demarcation. Others followed and settled in regions throughout British North America. North America was again reorganized and new political arrangements were made when Quebec was divided eight years later. The story of the great North American divide does not end here, but much of the remaining history is anticlimactic.

## Fixing the Border Forever

Since the American invasion in the War of 1812, Canada has not had to militarily defend its territory from its imperial neighbour. The Treaty of Ghent of 1814 attempted to define part of the boundary line between the US and British North America. In 1818 the western border was negotiated between Britain and Washington in London, not North America, and the resulting convention settled 1,372 kilometres of the boundary. In the far west, the US northern border was established not long after by the Oregon Treaty of 1846.[20] This makes the Canada-US border one of the earliest established and continuously recognized borders in the modern world. It is not the oldest though. The French-Spanish border, for example, was recognized by the Treaty of the Pyrenees, signed in 1659, and Sweden's boundary with Norway—part of Denmark at the time—one of the most stable in Europe, was drawn up in the 1740s.[21]

Neither Canadians nor Americans celebrate the date when their joint border was agreed upon. Canada did not have to adjust to a frontier arbitrarily imposed by Washington, nor did it ever close its frontier to the movement of people or goods from the Republic as a matter of economic principle for mercantilist reasons. At its origins, Canada was a commercial and settler colony born to trade. People, resources, investment flows and services have moved in both directions, sometimes easily, at other times with great difficulty, when the Republic and the Confederation used tariffs for nationalist ends. There were conflicts over Alaska at the turn of the twentieth century and tough words about free trade and access to each others' markets, but sovereign policies in an absolute way have never collided as they repeatedly have in Europe.[22]

Nor has US sovereignty ever been threatened by its northern neighbour. No US investors have faced a protectionist wall for very long. No Canadian government in the twentieth century has applied the kind of tough foreign ownership restrictions that would have kept Canada's resource bounty largely under Canadian control. Early in the nineteenth century Ontario introduced incentives to have logs processed in province, but most of the time all of Canada's national governments pursued foreign investors to transfer technology, jobs and production here.[23]

The establishment of the International Joint Commission (IJC) in 1909 further deepened the conviction that the Canada-US border was nonviolent and of low strategic order. Bureaucrats and diplomats were entrusted to settle conflicts related to water and other questions that arose, through compromise and consensus.

The politics of the Great Border were never the primary business of the IJC, a low-order body that only functioned well when US interests were not at stake. By then liberal nationalism had only two primary colours—market access and good neighbourliness—each a study in diplomacy and weakness. Canada's anxiety about gaining access to the US domestic market enabled smart and skilled US diplomats to extract concessions from their northern neighbour. This process of trade-offs and concessions took a quantum leap forward with the Ogdensburg Treaty signed in New York State in 1940.

Reading Mackenzie King's diary,[24] one would hardly know that the Canada-US relationship involved a foreign power. President Franklin D. Roosevelt phoned Prime Minister King and asked for a meeting the next day in Ogdensburg to work out the defence of the northern half of the continent. King agreed to meet and had no hesitation to accept without reservation the principle that Canada was part of the US security network. King signed the first of many joint defence undertakings that institutionalized cooperation between the two countries' military establishments. To enhance cooperation in the planning of sea, land, air and military productions, the Permanent Joint Defense Board was established, and the arrangements were formalized in the Hyde Park Declaration a year later. Here for some experts is the rather "unalarming" beginning of US homeland defence for the continent.

For King the logic of buying into continental security typified the mindset of his generation. He and his peers believed that they had to put as much diplomatic and economic distance between Canada and Britain as diplomatically possible, so Canadian independence meant coming closer to the US. His chief brain trust, O.D. Stelton, then undersecretary of state for External Affairs, believed in what he described as "a unique community of interests, perhaps even a collective identity" with Americans.[25] Their "big idea" (not unlike the similarly "big idea" currently being promoted by the C.D. Howe Institute and Canada's CEOs) was that US and Canadian military, defence, foreign policy and ultimately commercial policy had to be of one mind if Canada was to broaden its access to the US market and cement its friendship.

The historical record underlines just how erroneous this kind of policy was. Canadian elites were never convinced that the Canada-US border had much diplomatic or strategic value for Canadian domestic policy outside the economic realm. No one could ever imagine an American senior statesman dissing the border as a largely artificial creation, but for much of the time this was the prevalent attitude among many of Canada's leading diplomats. Hugh Keenleyside, one of Canada's senior officials, described the border in 1929 in deterministic terms, as "physically invisible, geographically illogical, militarily indefensible, and emotionally inescapable."[26] It is no wonder that, for all intents and purposes, the celebrated Canada-US border was not a priority in twentieth-century US history.

Ottawa's stance, heavy on pragmatism and short on strategic thinking, appeared to be relatively cost-free and seemingly natural, considering that Canada's territorial border wars with the US were all but settled by the twentieth century. The US invaded Cuba, Haiti and Mexico more than once and dispatched troops to Latin American countries on more than a dozen occasions. But these expansionist interventions failed to send a wake-up call to official Canada to rethink its role in the hemisphere. Canada did not produce the Canadian equivalent of a Charles Beard or a William Appleman Williams, historians who would educate two generations of Americans on the danger of empire. Harold Innis and Donald Creighton, both of whom had a commanding intellectual presence, never produced a systematic study of US power and its complex influence on Canadian cultural and political development. Europe would take the entire twentieth century to resolve territorial differences as nation-states looked to expand territorially—France wanted Alsace and Lorraine returned, Germany claimed its right to regain the territories lost in the 1919 peace settlement and the Soviet Union regarded its borders as inviolate. China and later India invested heavily in their borders diplomatically, skirmished militarily and went to war to establish a formal frontier.

In North America nothing like this transpired. The boundary question was essentially settled by unexciting diplomatic means that balanced state power with national ambition. Canada lost thirty acres to the US in 1925 following a minor adjustment of the border, and the US gained another 2.5 acres of water in a later adjustment, but the land border was seemingly irreversibly fixed for all time. Unlike Europe, Asia, Africa or Latin America, the two countries have not gone to war to defend or extend the border since it was established by the Oregon Treaty.[27] Canadian writers and historians have long romanticized it as "the most friendly and least visible line of international power in the world. It is crossed daily by thousands of travellers who hardly notice it in their passage." Bruce Hutchinson concluded his hymn-like praise by comparing the great frontier to "a Niagara of genial oratory ... illuminated ... by a perpetual diplomatic dialogue."[28]

## Internal Boundaries Are Also Vast
## but Different in One Critical Aspect

In its history, Canada has suffered from having too many borders, not too few. Its borders come in many shapes and sizes and many are internal. As immense as Canada's borders with the Republic are, its internal boundaries are equally vast. The Atlantic Ocean–Gulf of St. Lawrence shore is almost 30,000 km long. Canada's Pacific Ocean boundary is 16,000 km long, almost twice the Canada-US frontier. The Newfoundland–Atlantic Ocean–Gulf of St. Lawrence boundary stretches an awe-inspiring 18,000 km. In the far north, the Franklin District–Arctic Ocean–Davis Strait border is three-quarters the size of the Canada-US boundary. At the other extreme, the Nova Scotia–New Brunswick boundary is the smallest in the country, only thirty-four kilometres in length.

From another perspective, Canada is a victim of unbounded space. We have too much of it, as reflected in the immense size of Canada's political units. Our land and water perimeters amount to more than 61,000 km. Newfoundland's total land and water perimeter is 22,000 km, the largest in the entire northern Federation. British Columbia is next at 21,477 km, followed by the Northwest Territories and Quebec. Ontario is a small-shot, judged by its land and water perimeter, at only 6,200 km.[29]

Even with so many borders to maintain, Canada's spatial concept of the Great Border has always had a compelling quality, much more civic than driven by strict national security needs. Canadians have minimized its strategic dimensions and deepened its human security side as a domestic priority, reflecting the things Canadians share in common. We are one of the three large North American communities, whose loyalties are strongest within our own countries. We hardly register on each other's radar screens.

## The First Postmodern Border

For reasons specific to Canada, a belief in the country's distinctiveness has always occupied a large place in national mythology, far beyond the legal aspects of the border and the elite views of diplomats. When Canadians look into their history, they identify with the heroic voyages of the early explorers who took on the vast continent with its extremes of cold and danger. Follow the voyages of the early trappers and traders and, it is said by historians, you can see the broad outline of modern Canada's boundaries, *ad mari usque ad mare*. Such simplicity indeed. The expansion of the fur trade from east to west was the first transcontinental enterprise, but it was no more than a coincidence. The arrows of causality hardly begin to explain the origins of the modern Canada that would emerge some two hundred years later.

The truth was much more complex. Harold Innis' pivotal idea was that Canada was created because of geography and reinforced by the grooves of a transcontinental commerce, which served a basic collective need.[30] As D.W. Meinig points out, "every mature nation has its symbolic landscapes and these landscapes are an essential part of the symbolism of nationhood. The border and all that happens around it become a shared part of the ideas, memories and experiences that bind people together."[31] The border enters the ideological structures of the nation, vividly distinguishing "us from them," paves the way for the state to extend its power and authority over all individuals within its boundaries, and helps blur regional, ethnic, linguistic and class divides. The Canadian side was less rich in symbolism but nonetheless managed to play a transformative role in the imaginary notion of the nation.

In the twentieth century the most celebrated defining moment in the battle to establish the primacy of the Great Border in the Canadian national mindset was cultural, not economic. The first formative turning occurred during and immediately after World War I. Thousands of young Canadian soldiers came to the realization that we had grown far apart from the British. In the words of Frank Underhill, "Canadians went up Vimy Ridge as colonials and came down its bloody slopes as Canadians." Nationhood and nation-building were forged in wartime for Canadians at that "fatal ridge."[32]

The second formative moment occurred as American radio threatened to invade Canada in the thirties. Canadians could not compete with the cheap imports from NBC and other networks unless they pooled their resources and looked inwards to combat dominant US values and interests. Inspired in part by Walter Lippman's writing on democracy and public opinion, Graham Spry and others quickly understood that public broadcasting was the ideal instrument "to cultivate a healthy, alert, informed and active public opinion."[33]

## When the Border Mattered: Culture as Quasi-Sovereignty

The Radio League organized a hugely successful social movement for public broadcasting. The political climate persuaded Conservative, pro-business Prime Minister R.B. Bennett to establish the Canadian Broadcasting Corporation (CBC), a publicly funded authority that guaranteed citizens a democratic voice. It didn't ban private broadcasting but forced wealthy private broadcasters to compete with public authority with very relatively few resources. It was a typically soft-nationalist compromise supported by churches, trade unions, civic associations, some of the leading media, business groups and Quebec's opinion leaders, but flawed from its inception. US mass culture continues to pour into Canada through largely unregulated private broadcasters and the US film and music industry. Institutionally, the CBC, the Canada Council and the Canadian Radio-Television and Telecommunications

Commission (CRTC) remain a latter-day Maginot Line barely equipped to protect Canadian interests.

Still, because of turning points like these and the establishment of a non-American, publicly funded health care system, Canada's concept of the border has a "good citizen" quality to it. Anyone who doubts this should compare the Canadian and American customs declaration cards that must be completed by each visitor to the country. These seemingly insignificant instruments of border management tell a potent story.

## The Particularities of our Two Borders:
## Comparing Visa Entry Forms

On its customs declaration card, Canada Customs asks all visitors rather straightforward and obvious questions about firearms and other weapons, and goods that have commercial or professional value, which may require inspection. As an agricultural country, Canada asks its customs officials to demand that visitors declare anything that might threaten Canada's resource bounty, including animals, birds, insects, plants, soil, fruits, vegetables, meats, dairy products, living organisms or vaccines. Customs wants to know if you have purchased any articles made or derived from endangered species. The Canadian border is not presented as a defence perimeter as it is to the south. It is almost unseen by the visitor, a quick administrative inconvenience, something that matters only for immigration purposes. For a country with one of the longest borders in the world, Canadian officials convey the impression that, except for wrongful entry and illicit shipment of goods, the border operates as a kind of minor administrative irritant, and its physicality is almost rendered a moot point.

Should a Canadian plan to spend time in the United States, they immediately perceive a fundamental difference. The US border is highly politicized. The border official who greets you is armed and the border card for a visa waiver demands answers to a long list of probing questions.[34] A wrong answer and you could be detained, expelled or barred forever. The card asks whether you have been a drug abuser or an addict, or are infected with a communicable disease. It asks whether you have ever been arrested or convicted for a crime involving moral turpitude or a drug-related violation. It wants full disclosure on whether you have ever been arrested for two or more offences for which the aggregate sentence was five years or more. The United States expects full disclosure to the question that asks whether are you seeking entry to engage in criminal or immoral activities.[35]

US authorities have a particular interest in whether you were involved in any way with Nazi Germany and its allies, and whether you were prosecuted as a war criminal. They want full voluntary disclosure regarding any acts of espionage or sabotage, terrorist activity or genocide with no time limit imposed. US customs officials want to know if you have been excluded or deported from the United States or refused a visa for fraud or misrepresentation. American authorities have a massive computer data bank to double-check whether your answers are truthful and forthcoming. Visitors who have been detained previously or who have withheld custody of a child from a United States citizen granted custody of that child would be barred. Finally the form asks whether you have ever asserted immunity from prosecution, despite the fact that it is, of course, one's right to do so. For those with serious business, who intend to stay for more than a day of shopping, the border is the demarcation point that separates the American from the non-American, who is termed "an alien."

## The US Border as a National Institution

The US has always valued the border as a security ditch for protection and citizenship. Since the late 1990s the two have become increasingly tangled and next to impossible to separate. The American grand narrative has focused on a singular idea: the inevitable triumph of the US frontier over adversity, a vision that has no fixed territorial limits or spatial dimensions. Historically, it was pure nation-building given voice and respectability by historians and social reformers alike. The relentless expansion of the US meant that the frontier was always on the move. In the American mind, the US border/frontier was a marker and a perfect mirror of the American psyche.

There was precious little in the American psyche that was pan-American by intent or design. The myth was that all the people pouring into the US from Europe speaking so many different languages would embrace the American century and civic nationalism wholeheartedly. The "melting pot" is a singular image that speaks reams about the US meta-narrative. It was designed to fast-track monoculturalism and suppress the most visible forms of multiculturalism that immigrant societies naturally gravitate towards. The reality was always more complex.

Picture North America in the 1800s, a century before the monoculturalism of the US melting pot triumphed. Meinig provides the starting point to grasp just how far from its multicultural origins the continent has evolved under American interest and influence. He reminds us that Afro–North America stood at the southeast corner in an oblong shape that included Curaçao, Cuba, Jamaica and Florida, with New Orleans in the west and Bermuda as its eastern boundary. The British north was a vast territory from Hudson's Bay, butting up against Russian America in Alaska and bound by the enormous territory of Louisiana in the south. In the west, New Spain had claimed California and New Mexico as its own. Its territorial ambitions would collide with British North America in the northwest. On the political map of the time, the United States appeared as the least promising among the group. A hundred years later, expansion, conquest and the thirst for moving the frontier made Americans forgetful of the geopolitical diversity of the continent. They turned inwards as they moved aggressively to consolidate their power on the continent, and by the middle of the nineteenth century, diversity, the most important thread, had been dropped down two or three registers in importance.[36]

## The Restless US Frontier

Conquest and an unending obsession to move the frontier in all directions made Americans see the continent as an extension of their culture and values. Americans read the geography of the continent in terms of their own interests and put the full force of their nationalism behind the creed of US expansionism.[37] Fredrick Jackson Turner, arguably the most important American historian in shaping the American mind, singled out the frontier as the defining element in American individualism and popular democracy, and America's unique gift "to the garden of the world."[38]

During the nineteenth and early twentieth centuries, Turnerites published *The North American Review*, a New York-based magazine that caught the "Turner Wave" that was building at this time.

It presented articles on a wide variety of social, scientific, religious, economic, political, artistic and literary issues. However, the "North American" part of the title was a complete misnomer. Almost no mention was made of the "other" countries of North America, Canada and Mexico. Instead, the *Review* focused on US domestic issues, such as immigration, division of legislative powers, commercial expansion and the "Wild West," and presented articles on countries subject to direct American imperialism, such as Cuba and the Philippines. It provides us with an early example of the fragile and often absent North American perspective on the continent, its contributors and editors being more interested in events in the Pacific and west of the United States than those in their northern and southern backyards.

Although the facts behind Turner's "frontier thesis" did not make perfect sense and many of his claims were stylized generalizations that later American historians would demolish, his hypothesis has dominated American life to this day for a good reason: it became equated with the rise of self-confident US cosmopolitanism and fundamentalist patriotic values. From this angle, it is not difficult to grasp just how tendentious the idea of a culturally integrated North America was then and is still now.

In the rearview mirror of history, a single idea has stood out for Americans: Canada's West should be the US's north![39] Turner's notion of the frontier was a non-starter in Canada, given that the Canadian frontier was vaster, its climate harsher and the role of government greater than south of the border. For Canadians, nothing could be more preposterous than the idea that their wilderness was conquerable. Canada's wilderness remained defiant to mere human endeavour and required all the sovereign powers of the state to attempt to tame it. Market forces and geography combined to support a massive state presence in the economy, sharply differentiating Canada from the US model and its political culture.[40] For this reason alone there would be no replay of Turner's frontier thesis on the northern half of the continent, even though the constant movement of peoples across the permeable borders of the New World created communities of the like-minded.

## When the Border Doesn't Matter

The contemporary border/frontier continues to invoke different responses from Canadians and Americans. For Canadians it is about relations of power and the power differential between the two countries that constitute the Great Divide. For Canadians, social space, the nature of a spot or a place, is part of the material reality that structures human existence nationally, regionally and locally. Public places, markets, cultural centres, safe streets, clean cities, hospitals, universities and day care centres all need to be paid for and supported. But even more importantly, in the Canadian mind, social space is the result of collective endeavour. It is a large and visible part of Canada's patrimony, and Canadians have invested heavily in social space and the rights and obligations this entails. They believe that land and resources as well as education and health care are common property, public goods that form a large part of their heritage and should not be privately owned.[41]

Americans do not see the need for a public commitment of these resources. Meinig said it best of all: In the US, "landscape is wealth and space is a form of stored-up capital waiting to be exploited if the price is right. It is this fundamentalist view of space as a commercial frontier that continues to be so pre-eminent in contemporary American ideology and values."[42] The spin given by economic determinists is that the power differential is so large that Canada ought to throw in the towel. Popular commentary once claimed that North American economic integration would bind the national governments so tightly that autonomous public authority would expire.

Stephen Pearlstein, the *Washington Post*'s former Canadian correspondent, wrote as part of the end-of-Canada mentality, observing apocalyptically that "Canada is haunted by a disturbing question. Will there even be a Canada in 25 years, or will the country become, for all practical purposes, the 51st American state?"[43] This kind of morbid obsession about Canada as an improbable nation fails to explain the persistence of Canada as a separate but unequal entity or its prospects in the global economy.[44]

Significantly, no American believes that the US is going to disappear because of unparalleled levels of integration with Canada and Mexico. You will find no articles in the *New York*

*Times* or *Washington Post* on similar themes. Italians, who have as fragile a country as Canada in many important respects, do not have this sort of fear. French intellectuals do not rush to declare solemnly that "the possibility of France not mattering has to be taken seriously." Nor are many much poorer countries, with few of Canada's resources, obsessed with the possibility of wholesale assimilation by a powerful neighbour. Quebec intellectuals have never embraced fatalism and the end of politics; rather, in the modern period, these notions have triggered resistance and pushed Quebecers to develop strategies to level the playing field. What is at the source of so much border angst on the English side of the language divide?

There is a fundamental misconception about border culture and border regions in North America. At the border, cultures are mixed and traits exchanged, but goals and values are not always automatically blurred as many contend. People living at the frontier end up straddling two cultures without any definitive resolution. Take the well-known example of law and order in our two Wests. The settlement of the two North American Wests went in fundamentally different directions with immediate conse-quences. In British Columbia and the Canadian West generally, there was "no revolvering, no instance or need of lynch law."[45] The North West Mounted Police provided control for the Okanagan and Red River valley districts. Just across the line, rampant individualism and lawlessness prevailed as there were few police to establish the authority of the US state. What this tells us, as Klein observed, is that social interaction "does not lead to the disappear-ance or assimilation of the cultures." [46] Regional identity, no less than national identity, needs boundary markers and national institutions and values to fill this function.[47]

Some of the boundaries are lines on a map while others are linguistic or cultural divides. When we think of places, such as Toronto, Vancouver, L.A., New York and Mexico City, with diverse cultures co-existing among different neighbourhoods, the boundaries are cultural rather than territorial. So boundaries and borders of a non-state variety are also created by the presence or lack of communication and social networks where people meet and congregate.

## When Culture Crosses the Border:
## Canada's Un-American Narrative

In a global world, few borders are airtight and there are always spill-overs between neighbouring countries, states and provinces—francophones in Maine, Hispanic-Americans, the North American West. The shared experiences of the frontier—migration, existence on the periphery, often speaking a common language, labouring as farmers and settlers—have all stamped the borderlanders' perspective with shared identities and aspirations, irrespective of which side of the border they live on. In terms of lived experience, the border becomes a "spatial record" of the relationship between local communities and their national government. It produces oddities such as Stanstead, a border town of about three thousand on the Quebec-Vermont frontier where the water and sewer systems are shared, but not values, perceptions and loyalties. After Ottawa's decision not to back Bush's "coalition of the willing," the library that straddles the frontier was declared a no man's land. The citizens of Stanstead struggle not to criticize each other "because we are all neighbours. Our kids play hockey together." But when the chips are down, of course, the border matters and if you cross CANUSA, its main street, you are expected to report to the border control![48] Even in small towns like Stanstead, the differences between Canadians and Americans are palpable and deep.

As an exercise in geopolitics, the full chronology of the Canada-US border has yet to be written. Even though there are many border issues, the fact that no Canadian government has developed a strategic plan to manage its side of the fence speaks volumes about our mentality and our perception of the great southern border. In 1917, James Macdonald wrote a prescient book significantly entitled, *The North American Idea,* based on lectures he gave at Vanderbilt University. It can be read as the definitive Canadian answer to the great American historian Turner. Macdonald put his primary argument bluntly: the North American idea is "the right of a free people to govern themselves"; North America was about "national integrity as an inalienable right."[49] How Canadian to defend sovereignty for all countries both great and small, and how unlike Turner's restlessly moving frontier big idea!

Macdonald's big idea was to make "every little nationality ... secure against the ambition and greed of the large and the powerful."[50] His North America was identified with freedom, self-criticism and tolerance, not the American-style frontier. It was about the relationship between immigration and assimilation, multiculturalism and monoculturalism, cooperation and unilateralism, and an array of questions relating to pluralism, nationalism and federalism. Above all else, it was about the capacity to be different and yet remain interdependent, like the directions of a compass. Post-9/11, Canada and the United States have yet to find that balance between diversity, citizenship and social need north and south of the Great Divide. We have reached a turning point where the political geography of the continent has changed beyond all recognition.

# 3. TIPPING POINT:
## THE NEW POLITICAL GEOGRAPHY

> "Canada and Mexico may seek partners; the United States seeks only customers." —John Wirth, from "Advancing the North American Community"

## The Regional Lock-In

As legal and spatial boundaries have been redefined by new information technologies, does it make sense to regard the continent as an incipient nation-in-waiting when there are so many sub-national and sub-regional identities operating within each country? Experts have never agreed on the precise characteristics of a regional economy and its effect on regional integration and development. If the defining characteristic is not exports as a percentage of GDP, are there twelve regions or forty? Is it fair to talk about Michigan, Illinois and Ohio and their own histories and local economies in the same breath as Quebec, Ontario and B.C.?

Ontario and Quebec comprise large sub-economies, as do California and New York, but their populations are worlds apart, with strong sub-regional political cultures. The micro-regional culture of upstate New York shares nothing in common with northern Ontario other than the fact that Canada's massive energy exports light and heat much of the "Empire State." Economically, New York and Big Sur in California are far apart, but this is less important than the fact that middle-brow Americans from the east and west coasts share a common value system, believing in the supremacy of American individualism and democracy. The majority of Americans no longer vote, but this has not diminished their faith in the uniqueness of American values.

So far no one has been able to give a definitive answer to the question of the nation-region interface. Should it be defined by production networks that traverse the continent? Or should the growing volume of goods and services that flow between metropolitan cities be the defining standard? Or is North America morphing into a vast hinterland of metropolitan centres dominated by New York, Los Angeles, Toronto and Montreal? Surprisingly, North Americans remain markedly attached to their national communities despite the transnational flow of commerce, information and culture. We are more Canadian than ever in our values, as Michael Adams has powerfully demonstrated in his book, *Fire and Ice*.[1] Values are the litmus test of similarity and sameness. We are becoming more unlike despite NAFTA, deficit cutting and the rise of the neo-conservative right.

No one can dispute that Americans are more committed to their country and flag than at any time in recent history. The Pew 2003 Global Values and Attitudes Survey reconfirms, if any confirmation is required, that 75 percent of Americans were pro-US values and policies in world affairs. In most other countries those interviewed were critical of their government and society. Not so in the US. Americans have become the statistical outlier in their global views of others and themselves.

Still as Newfoundlanders, Californians, New Yorkers, Torontonians and Haligonians, a part of us likes to romanticize the local and assert our unique regional identities and lifestyles. We want to view the region separately from the nation-state and give it the power and autonomy the nation-state once had. In the end, North Americans are often of the same species but decidedly not of the same family. There are divides that can't be easily set aside or ignored.

A hundred years ago, close to one-quarter of Canadians born in Canada were living in the US. A century later only about two percent live on the other side of the border. The vast majority have chosen to remain at home as the two countries have grown ever closer economically.[2] The sole exceptions are managers, executives and skilled professionals who have used the NAFTA temporary work visa to find employment in the US. On average about 16,000 leave each year, but many return.

Just prior to the signing of the NAFTA, Canada barely registered on the US migratory map. A puny 7,100 Americans chose to make

Canada their home each year between 1991 and 1994.[3] In 1997 an Industry Canada survey found that 1,866 managers and 916 engineers and computer scientists took up permanent residency in the US, and more than 500 nurses and almost 400 doctors also moved south. The more skilled have the best chance to get a US green card to work legally. Certainly there is no Niagara of movement from the US across the "open" border post-NAFTA.[4]

## North America's Nation-Centred Regionalism

All of North America's regions remain stubbornly nation-centred and dependent on state and provincial authorities on their side of national borders. The Foundry, or Great Lakes, region is probably the most successful industrial area on the continent. Anchored in the mass-production industries of automobiles, steel, chemicals and electronics, it stretches between Chicago, Toronto and Ottawa anchored in middle America and central Canada. It is driven by the dense concentration of industry in south-central Ontario, as well as intrastate commerce in parts, machinery and equipment among Michigan, Illinois and Ohio. This industrial heartland is a dynamic and wealthy region.

No other part of North America has as much interstate and interprovincial trade as the Foundry. Despite the gravity model findings of Helliwell and McCallum, Ontario trades more with the Foundry than with any other province—95 percent of Ontario's exports are shipped to the US and almost 80 percent of US-based multinationals operate from the golden triangle of south-western Ontario. From a Canadian perspective, Ontario is the industrial, financial and technological centre of Canada's most modern and competitive industries. Its industries are sophisticated and successful. From a North American perspective, Ontario is a small player dwarfed by the rest of the vast American consumer and industrial economy. It is linked by commerce to the Great Lakes region, but politically and culturally it remains distinct, as Ontarians are also strong nationalists and provincialists. Its political culture is a confused blend of red Tory and social democratic values mixed with a liberal market individualism dominated by the branch-plant mentality of its managers and much of the economic elite.

Think of it this way. Being close to the US doesn't mean that

Ontarians have the whole world lying just beyond their border; they only have an easily accessed corner. Most of the US market is very far from Ontario's industries. Canada's GDP is only about 10 percent of the North American total, and the entire Canadian economy is about the size of the GDP of Texas, according to Earl Fry, one of the US's top Canadian experts.[5] The economy of New York State is the size of Brazil's; Turkey's the size of Washington State's, and France's is equal to California's. Successful countries have diversified their exports to the US; Canada has not and in the main continues to excel in traditional exports such as rocks, logs, energy, agricultural products and auto parts. So, being in the backyard of the US market has not dramatically changed the composition of Canadian exports across the board. Canada is losing out on higher valued exports as the gap between total exports and the share of highly processed value added exports as a percentage of GDP has more doubled since 1990.[6] We sell a lot because US companies operate on both sides of the border line. Over 50 percent of our merchandise exports are intra-firm.

Like all industrialized countries, Canada has relied on government initiatives and strategies to develop an international-scale economy, which has benefited most leading Canadian companies, even if they would be the last to admit it. Nationalistic policies, such as the Canada-US Auto Pact, signed in 1965, and the Maquiladora Program initiated by Mexico in the 1980s with strong support from the US State Department and US big-three auto assemblers, were key in altering the division of labour among North America's car industries, plants and regional producers. It is no coincidence that the best deals Canada and Mexico ever struck, for a big-time market niche in the continental car production market, were these nation-to-nation deals negotiated with Washington.

In a free trade age, with so many different strategies in play, the state has continued to play an interventionist role of some kind throughout North America. Governments make a difference even if their policies are not always very innovative. US military bases and other kinds of defence spending on infrastructure provide local job and work opportunities for hundreds of thousands of Americans in the poorest regions. North of the forty-ninth parallel, the Maritimes region, by dint of provincial government subsidies and handouts, has the distinction of being one of the continent's leading-edge call centres for US multinationals and service industries. Some 35,000 people work as customer representatives in call centres in Nova Scotia and New Brunswick. The stress is high and the wages are low, at about $9 an hour. This kind of part-time, contract work is replacing fish processing plants as the region's chief low-wage employer. The role of government has been critical and decisive in the Maritimes, creating some of the most important opportunities for private entrepreneurs.[7]

In Quebec, too, government grants are the source of many new jobs in the service and high-tech sectors. Bombardier, a global success story, has received billions in subsidies from both Ottawa and Quebec to sell its short takeoff and landing airplanes.[8] Quebec has pioneered Quebec Inc., a strategy it used to great advantage in the 1960s and 1970s, creating dynamic and aggressive state enterprises for Quebecers and an emerging francophone middle class. The Caisse de Dépôt has become one of the continent's premier investors, with funds totaling over $130 billion in 2003. It uses Quebec's pension plan savings and other public funds to invest in high-profile industrial enterprises in Quebec and throughout the world.

By contrast, market forces left on their own have proven to be poor instruments for delocalizing highly regionalized economies. New innovations and growth in economies of scale favour already privileged regions. Knowledge spill-overs between firms in such famed clusters as California's Silicon Valley and Boston's Route 128 have created a unique, internationally competitive advantage for many high-tech firms, but local considerations remain as determinant as ever for existing industries. Take, for example, the cases of financial services in New York, film production in Los Angeles, and textiles in the US Southwest. Strong local factors supported and sustained their comparative advantages. To this day, Wall Street nominates three representatives to the Federal Reserve Bank and ensures New York's commanding role as the centre of finance.[9] The L.A.-centred movie industry has received all kinds of critical support in financial and labour regulation from the California state legislature to maintain its dominance as a production centre. Textile giants in the US Southwest have benefited from low-wage and anti-labour state legislation. Most critically, every American industrial lobby group relies on US trade law to protect jobs and investments from unwanted import competition.

All of these dynamic forces have prevented any reshuffling of the cards among American and Canadian regional competitors.[10] Canadian firms are viewed as savvy and smart but only second-string players in the highly efficient US regional system of growth and rapid industrial change. They haven't the clout of French, German or Japanese megacorporations. What's prevented Canada from moving up the regional ladder, if we take seriously the proposition that North America is an incipient region-state?

## An Historical Puzzle: US Development and Locational Choices

The best American economic geographers have explained that divergent regional development in North America is driven by cumulative processes that pervasively influenced national economies from the mid-1800s to the 1960s. Paul Krugman argues convincingly that the concentration of industries in the United States was locked in early on and was not strictly driven by demand or comparative advantage. Location of demand became a highly conservative force, freezing in time an established centre-periphery pattern that lasted "intact into the next century."[11]

It is not incidental that the US eastern seaboard maintained its industrial dominance even when its primary market had moved west and its resources had to be trucked in. The end result was that the American West failed to develop manufacturing even when a larger local market existed and could have supported it. The US manufacturing belt remained concentrated in a narrow stretch of territory along the eastern seaboard long after the centre of gravity of agricultural and mineral production moved west.

This story is complex, but it contains important lessons for North America today. Imagine Canada and the US as a multiregional economy where the border is neutral and Canada has a very small share of the population, and the US the majority of people. Markets are always difficult to exploit because manufacturers will only locate in markets that are not necessarily larger but better known to them and where industries obtain strong economies of scale by investing in best practice technology. Just as often they prefer the advantages offered by local labour markets over distant ones. American regionally based growth poles act as powerful magnets for capital, talent, expertise and new technology to move among regions and mostly within national borders. Only under special conditions will industry relocate to take advantage of potentially new economies of scale. American industry migrated to Canada in record numbers to gain access to British imperial markets, particularly after World War I. They used Canada as a platform to export to South Africa, Australia and the UK, with great success.

The history of North American regional development in the contemporary period has followed this well-established trajectory. Other than auto assemblers and parts suppliers, firms tend to bunch up on their side the border and stay put. They don't pull up roots to exploit new market opportunities elsewhere on the continent unless they have to. The most competitive and mobile US giants go overseas or elsewhere in the hemisphere. In the big picture, some industries and firms migrate, like auto parts manufacturers, but most don't leave their regional home base unless there are powerful forces driving them outside the region. They tend to stick to their original sites long after there is any need to. They are not cross-border hoppers by instinct, doing so only when it is in their interest to gain a specific advantage from new technology, as now.

This kind of corporate behaviour focuses the mind on an essential point, that regional divergence cannot be explained by standard equilibrium equations in which all of North America's regions are on a level playing field for new investment. A different set of dynamics is operating regionally and nationally. The most important is that the US manufacturing beltways of the continent have always fuelled the dynamism of the American economy in the aggregate.[12] The above-average performances of America's national regional champions have followed a well-documented pattern of sucking in investment and developing impressive economies of scale, but always at a price.

## Failed American Regions and the Race to Be Competitive

The continent's poorly positioned regions not only fail to be competitive and diversify exports, but fall further behind in the race to upgrade. The poorest American states have been failed economic zones for as long as Newfoundland has been the poorest region in North America. They have never gotten a better deal by opening their markets to international forces. Incomes are low and these regions or states have always had the largest number of poor and low-income families on the continent. Nebraska, Kansas, Mississippi, West Virginia, South Dakota and Arkansas are at the bottom of US per capita income measures and neither federal nor local tax breaks, reliance on free trade or other corporate subsidies have ever changed very much in these poorest US regions. Flexible accumulation strategies have failed to make a dent in breaking the regional poverty cycle even though the US has had the lowest unemployment rates and almost three decades of above average job growth among OECD countries.

It is no coincidence that many of the poorest US states have abolished personal income tax or instituted a flat-rate tax. According to the Washington-based Institute on Taxation and Economic Policy, "their tax systems take a much greater share of income from middle- and low-income families than from the wealthy."[13] Some of the most regressive state tax systems, and lowest wage rates, in the US are found in the industrial heartland, in states such as Illinois, Michigan, Pennsylvania and secondary-rank assemblers such as Tennessee. Among the have-not states it is not uncommon that people at the bottom 20 percent by income pay up to five and a half times more of their earnings in taxes than the wealthy do.

With few of its federal programs addressing the growth in poverty since the US welfare state began to shrink in the 1980s, American poverty rates are among the highest of any industrial country. This is the primary finding of the Luxembourg income study, which examined poverty rates for eleven industrialized countries, employing a standard of 40 percent of median income as the benchmark. Researchers found that in 1997 the US had the highest poverty rate, at 10.7 percent. Canada, with regional unemployment compensation programs, more generous social policies and higher social-assistance minimums came in at a distant 6.6 percent.[14]

## America's Postmodern Narrative of *La Frontera*

America's failed regions —Alabama, South Dakota or Arkansas, to name only a few—loom large in the postmodern narrative of pluralistic experiences as places inhabited by the outsider, the excluded, the oppressed and the marginal. Here the highest proportion of poorly paid employees inhabit the borderland, "a vague and undetermined place."[15] They are not part of the Krugman story about regional upgrading through dynamic change and industrial inventiveness. They haven't made the grade but nonetheless occupy a special place in American mythology.

The southwestern border particularly dominates the American imagination as one of the most important regions in the modern US narrative. When Americans write about *la frontera*, "a narrow strip along a steep edge," in the powerful imagery of Kerwin Lee Klein, as a place where they encounter the other and process those differences, it is always as a tale of their own frontier and ethnocentric history.[16] It is a narrative of exclusion or assimilation that springs directly from an obsession with the frontier as part of the American dream.

The American appetite for frontier history, though vast and unlimited, is marked by one primary colour. It is always US-centric and focused on the need to enhance America's awareness of its own internal cultural boundaries. From James Ellroy's cult novels of US power, violence and criminality, to Russel Banks' powerful indictment in *Continental Drift,* works of surreal fiction epitomize the anomie of contemporary American regional society. They are stories of broken-down tough guys and pathological killers locked in a permanent war against nature and the US state. These social misfits are at the margin of the marginal economies.

## Canada as Ethno-History: America's Blind Spot

Canada cannot be typecast as an "edge region" of North America. Canadians belong neither to the world of the excluded nor the assimilated, nor are we an outlaw people, defiant and unruly. Hence we protrude like an outcropping in the American landscape, uninteresting as ethno-history to the American mind. Canada is not an integral and recognized part of the US regional universe. The exception is Quebec, an exotic head-turner compared to English Canada, the "plain Jane," dull and Americanized.

Frequently the Maritimes, the dutiful daughter, gets better press as a different, friendlier kind of edge region—with its old-fashioned liberal values of decency, community and individualism. These caricatures cannot be read literally, but they make a basic point. Canadians do not fit the defining characteristic of the prototypical American frontier experience, where the frontier always extinguishes cultural differences in the name of a new cosmopolitan future.

In the American imagination, Canada has never existed or needed to be assessed because it is there and part of the larger context that has to be taken into account.[17] To paraphrase McLuhan, Canadians have a deeply rooted libertarian streak in their national character. When urban Canadians go out "to answer the call of the wild" as North Americans, McLuhan felt we did so with a private face and often a private voice: "Our individual life is hidden away for private judgement rather than public inspection."[18] We are hardly visible to the US cultural eye and have rarely fulfilled the dramatis personae that Harold Innis, Canada's most innovative political economist, foresaw for Canada on the periphery of US power. In his evocative words, frontier economies, such as Canada's, were slated to become "storm centres to the modern international political economy."[19]

He was wrong in this important insight into the Canada-US relationship. In the twentieth century, Canada never became an articulate centre of opposition to US power. The insurgent tradition of resistance that he predicted failed to materialize, and Canada with its truncated economy never saw the need to develop a full range of effective economic policies with which to constrain US influence in its domestic affairs. More importantly, social policy has been the single area of distinction in which Canada has excelled since the 1970s, though not without a chequered history.

Why was Canada more innovative in the domain of social policy than in the arena of international competitiveness? The identical Canadian mindset was not motivated to invest in a national system to innovate technology. At other times, Ottawa saw the need for a broad-based unemployment insurance system but not for legislation to require Canadian employers to invest in skills training across key industrial sectors. Here is a puzzle that needs answers and links back to the issues Krugman so powerfully analyzed. Immigration, public goods and geography often work in ways that reinforce Canada's capacity to be different in North America. Well before the signing of NAFTA, in the early part of the twentieth century, the primary business of the national government was investing in ports, railways, harbours and roads. Tariffs were needed to protect Canada's infant industry and create work and employment before the welfare state was established after World War II. Since the 1990s, spending on infrastructure has become a shadow of what it once was. Spending on roads and other infrastructure has fallen to about 5.5 percent of GDP, about one-half the levels in the golden era of Canadian capitalism in the 1960s and 1970s.[20]

As the flows of Canadian immigration have changed, Canadian citizenship issues demand much more from public authority, in terms of both public goods and policies of social inclusion to promote multiculturalism, or what experts prefer to call "diversity through shared institutions and values." The complex needs of the demanding Canadian citizenship agenda contests a narrow reading of economic issues and in recent times has become one of the transversals of modern political life, challenging the rigid Left-Right alignment of Canadian politics

## Citizenship, Identity and Markets

Since the late 1980s, identity politics have required that Ottawa protect Canada's multicultural diversity much more aggressively and rivalled any incipient belief that the regions of the continent were coming together as a social entity. Canadian multiculturalism, as it evolved, forced Canada to look inwards rather than outwards and take stock of a much larger transformative process than any group of NAFTA effects.

The concept of "multicultural" was based on the principle that no one group takes precedence over any other—all identities are in theory equal and the government welcomes and encourages active citizenship. Multiculturalism has been a process and not a one-shot deal. New Canadians have had to be given the "opportunity and capacity to participate in the shaping of their communities and their country."[21] So, far from being a one-track minimalist liberal creed tied to market fundamentalism, diversity and citizenship have infused Canadian society with a big-idea agenda that has had to be managed by Ottawa, the provinces and cities. Immigrants have needed to be housed, helped with job searches and often retrained, helped to master a language and have education provided for their kids.

The Multiculturalism Act of 1988, enacted barely a year after the signing of the first free trade agreement, commits the federal government to protect ethnic diversity, ensure equal employment opportunities in federal institutions and establish policies and programs that develop active citizens who will shape the future of Canada and their communities. Continued changes in immigration patterns in the late 1970s shifted attention towards visible minority groups and race relations in Canada, as an increasing number of non-white immigrants entered the country. Human rights and employment equity became priority concerns, as were social issues such as the media's depiction of minorities. It was during this period that statute, constitutional and international law expanded markedly; most notable in the national context were the Citizenship Act of 1977, the Canadian Human Rights Act of 1977 (revised 1985), the Canadian Charter of Rights and Freedoms of 1982, the Employment Equity Act of 1986 and the Multiculturalism Act of 1988.[22]

In Canada, citizenship is anchored in the nation, and constitutional citizenship is protected by Canada's Charter of Rights and Freedoms. Section 27 instructs judges to interpret the Charter "in a manner consistent with the preservation and enhancement of the multicultural heritage of Canadians." In theory, immigration and diversity needs cannot be easily overridden or ignored even in a free trade era.[23]

In fact, Ottawa spends a pittance on official multiculturalism in comparison to its support for bilingualism, the program that has always taken the lion's share of federal funding in this area. Support for ethnic organizations has always been modest, and it is unclear how much of a difference Ottawa's policies have made. What is not in doubt is that Canadian diversity has had to be recognized and accepted. Since the early days popular support for the idea of diversity and multiculturalism has acquired as much strength outside Ottawa as in the corridors of government.

Because Canada has never had a strong "I am Canadian" culture, Canada immigrants and newcomers have not been expected to assimilate into the culture of the majority to be Canadian. How could it be otherwise? For reasons indigenous to Canada, this pluralist conception of the national community has given the politics of citizenship a great deal of room to grow. This has meant that Canadians and Quebecers have had to devise institutions that construct a more differentiated identity, one based on a very strong belief in pluralism, tolerance and fairness, rather than on a rigid common public culture. Danielle Juteau is right that it was Jacques Parizeau's attack on "ethnics" for the 1995 referendum loss that forced Quebecers to bury the old Quebec nationalism and extend the boundaries of the national community to all residents.[24]

The Charter requires Ottawa to protect diversity, remove racial, ethnic and gender barriers to inclusion, and ensure in legal terms that new immigrants have wide access to society's resources and benefits. Charter activism has not forced Ottawa to do all that it should, but the Charter has created high public expectations that a strong state presence is a social good and the proper role for government. It has also made Canada's border policies a beltway that determines who enters Canada and has a right to settle here and be part of Canadian society.

## Global Cultural Flows and the Transformation of Canada

Surprisingly, public policy experts have been slow to grasp the dramatic impact of the global flow of immigrants, which has become an unstoppable dynamic in recent times. It has challenged the commerce-first border with its belief that border issues between Canada and the US had been all but settled by free trade.

Global immigration flows into Canada have broken all past records. Immigrants are coming to Toronto from China (21 percent), India (17 percent), Pakistan (9.2 percent) and the Philippines (6 percent). Korea, the United Arab Emirates, Iran, Saudi Arabia and Romania comprise another 10 percent. Vancouver, Montreal and Winnipeg are other epicentres of immigration. In 2003, China became the leading country for immigration to Canada. Even smaller cities that used to be outside the multicultural flow are receiving immigrants from these countries. The percentage of foreign-born Canadians has reached its highest level in seventy years at 18.4 percent. Only Australia, with 22 percent, exceeds this. [25]

Today's immigrants are more skilled than any group of immigrants in recent times. Although they often come from lower-income families, they have the support of their family and tight-knit immigrant communities. They have the drive and skills needed to negotiate the demands of their new society. According to the most recent census, the sons and daughters of immigrants are better educated and more likely to go to university than native-born Canadians. Immigrant offspring are highly concentrated in the most skilled occupations, gravitating towards the natural or applied sciences, health care and the financial sector. Immigrant young adults aged twenty to twenty-nine form the largest age group.

As outsiders in their new country, first-generation immigrants have faced barriers that every immigrant group traditionally experiences on arrival. They have to take the low-paying jobs, and many are de-skilled. For example, many South Asian and Middle Eastern immigrants' higher-education credentials are not recognized by Canadian authorities. But they have not encountered permanent silos of racism and exclusion. Their skills and education provide them with resources to get ahead.[26] These transformative global cultural flows have become, in ways no one predicted, more important and far-reaching for Canadian society than even a decade of free trade and spending cutbacks. Trade has not inspired any great sense of national achievement, but identity and citizenship have captured Canada's political imagination on both sides of the Quebec/Ontario border.

In the minds of new Canadians, identity is a source of pride, linked to the integrity of territory and the collective "we" of public space. A *Globe and Mail* poll, conducted by the Centre for Research and Information on Canada, found that second-generation Canadians in their twenties ranked multiculturalism and the Charter of Rights and Freedoms as the highest sources of Canadian pride.[27]

In ways that no expert could have predicted, Canadian immigrants have bought into the citizenship and identity agenda in record numbers. It is not the official programs alone that explain the unprecedented response. The numbers tell us one significant fact, and that is that Canadian citizenship has appreciated massively in value.[28] It is sought-after and prized. In the 1970s, 60 percent of adult immigrants became citizens; by 2000, naturalization levels had risen to over 70 percent. In the US, the naturalization rate has taken a nose-dive, plummeting from a buy-in of just over 60 percent in 1970, to 35 percent in 2000, the lowest in a hundred years. Why are there such fundamental differences and a clearly identifiable citizenship gap?

## The End of Welfare as We Knew It

Prior to 1996 there were two established welfare states in North America, but in 1996, almost a decade after Ottawa had passed its Multiculturalism and Citizenship Act, Clinton terminated Aid to Families with Dependent Children, the legislation that provided entitlements to needy families and was the cornerstone of the US welfare state. US welfare had been inclusive. Immigrants, legal residents and the recently arrived had all qualified for support and assistance. Clinton replaced the previous legislation with the Personal Responsibility and Work Opportunities Reconciliation Act (PRWORA).[29]

The redefinition of US citizenship shot to the top of the policy agenda. By the late 1990s, for the first time a sharp distinction was being drawn between citizen and immigrant, and deserving and undeserving citizens.[30] Permanent residents were to be denied access to health insurance, nutrition benefits, welfare and related work supports. In addition, they are not entitled to aid for the aged and disabled. It was estimated that the US government would save $20 billion from these restrictions alone.[31]

The PRWORA focused on workfare, tough rules and harsh penalties, imposing two-year time limits on eligibility to benefits with an overall five-year lifetime limit. This watershed reform legislation cut the legs off of all existing social programs, setting new eligibility requirements and forcing every state to maintain a balanced budget. The psychology of the program succeeded in ways that no other reform legislation in the last forty years had. It was the tipping point that would redefine North America's institutional character and, just as importantly, America's level of collective engagement in civic responsibility.

With the formal end of the US welfare state, individual states were free to impose their own carrots and sticks, and to make rules tougher and more restrictive. Many states imposed even tougher eligibility requirements, harsher penalties and stiffer work requirements, including restrictions on having children while receiving welfare. Welfare recipients who had additional children lost their welfare benefits. Social workers in many states were given incentives to reduce the welfare roles even further. The new legislation reduced the numbers on welfare by almost 50 percent.[32] In addition, PRWORA denied lawful immigrants eligibility to certain benefits and gave states the capacity to withhold other benefits to immigrants until they became citizens. Immigrants became by default or design one of the prime targets of a government-led revolution to redefine American citizenship practices to fit market fundamentalist principles and the conservative social revolution.

Under a waiver program, states could impose much tougher rules than were contained in the original legislative proposal. Over thirty states took advantage of this "flexible provision" to introduce departures from past practices. The number of families covered by US welfare benefits dropped precipitously from 4.5 million in 1996 to 2.25 million in 2000. Single mothers, disadvantaged mothers and those with the lowest employment skills left the welfare rolls in large numbers. Most had no choice given the tough rules and incentives to slim welfare rolls. North America has never witnessed such a disenfranchisement from welfare benefits in such a short period of time.[33]

The spending cuts that US states were forced to make fell heavily on low-income workers who had lost their jobs, and permanent residents and recently arrived immigrants who were without resources. With so many applicants, many stop-gap social welfare programs have gone over budget. They provide minimal support, but there are simply too many poor people for many states to cope with the demand. In 2002, forty states had to battle budgetary shortfalls amounting to nearly $40 billion. The outlook for state budgets was recently described as "bleak" and "dire" by US governors, who called for billions of dollars in new federal support.

It is an understatement to say that distributional issues do not rate highly in Washington's policy analysis circles. Decentralization was designed, in the words of Alice Rivlin, the former director of the Office of the Budget and now a senior fellow at the Brookings Institution, "to end the growing sense of powerlessness" that the average American feels.[34] The neo-conservative revolution stressed devolution and not the need for deepening and broadening federal social programs that had already been cut back, and access to them narrowed. But this primary goal, commanding citizen loyalty, has not been achieved by devolving government responsibilities to the state level.

The radical decentralization of education, health, social welfare and medicaid has created confusion between the federal and state governments over functions and responsibilities. This stands in contrast to Canadian federalism, which has a much clearer division of powers. Ottawa's redistributive powers are large and highly visible to any Canadian living in a have-not region. Transfer payments from wealthy to the less-well-off provinces run into billions of dollars annually and equalization payments are part of the constitutional deal struck by Trudeau when the Constitution was repatriated in the early 1980s. In Canada's federal system, the boundary lines are sharp, even if the overlaps are large. In the US, local and state governments are unwilling to take unpopular measures such as raising taxes to reduce income inequality. The political forces against tax increases are as strong in state capitals as in Washington.[35] Washington's redistributive role is tiny compared to Ottawa's, and American states have far fewer jurisdictional powers than Canadian provinces possess.

In its present state the US system reduces any possibility of political renewal and makes US politics least responsive to the needs of low-income Americans. It wasn't always a system of indifference, but it certainly has become one since the Reagan revolution in the 1980s. Currently the US federal system is overstretched and in deficit position at both the state and national levels because of deep tax cuts introduced in recent times by all levels of government. The consequence is that with less revenues there is little spending room for redistributive social programs. In the recent period, state spending has risen twice as fast as federal domestic spending.[36] Without the resources to match, and forbidden by federal law to run a deficit, more than forty state governments have cut services, fired state employees and imposed new flat-rate taxes, a burden that falls most heavily on low-income Americans. It is projected that by 2004 the American deficit will reach a record high level of more than five percent of GDP. The size of the deficit, including the hefty bill for the US occupation of Iraq, will mean new cuts to social spending and other areas of the budget or, failing that, an even larger national deficit.

## The New Contract with America

Some American pundits have called these sweeping changes a "new citizenship," "the contract with America" or, simply, ultra-liberalism, although not of the cruder kind associated with free trade. It is a potent revision because citizenship is always tied to the nation-state's territoriality and its exclusionary capacity. When there is an external threat, American nationalism has become inseparable from the template idea expressed in Clinton's first inaugural address of "one America," "the world's indispensable nation." What makes this latest expression of American nationalism so singular as a political creed is that the foreigner is increasingly viewed as a menace to national security. Crime prevention, enforcement of existing legislation and coordinating information among police agencies, intelligence and immigration officials reveal the functionality of borders for security purposes. The disjuncture between security and US citizenship is now very large.

The inspiration for drawing the line between the citizen and immigrants for federal programs is a pure nineteenth-century liberal model—only the deserving are to be considered part of society. Centralized public structures of the modern welfare state are relegated to the sidelines and in its place "smaller, more private, more local forms of organization are to be admired."[37] This notion is derived from Madison's idea that no majority should be able to dominate society. The only way to guard against the vice of majority rule, according to Karl Rove, the brain trustee for Bush and the Republican Party, is to break society into "so many parts, interests and classes of citizens" that the rights of individuals will never be threatened by any combination of the majority. How un-Canadian and so far removed from a public culture of common responsibility.

It is a peculiar vision of society where the aggregate interests of the community barely exist in any recognizable form and where the social bond is reduced to a bundle of legal rights and competing interests in the hope that no one group or interest will ever become too dominant, powerful or influential. For Rove and Bush the best society is "the one in which many groups compete and counterbalance each other, to the point of perfect political equipoise."[38]

No other society on the planet shares this communitarian ideal of politics to an equivalent degree. The success of moral conservatism in the US goes far beyond Bush's presidential victory. It aims to displace the once mighty Democrats, who dominated US national political life from Roosevelt through Clinton, as the governing coalition. Canada has never had the capacity to engineer systemic social change without regard for outcomes on such an unparalleled scale. Quebec nationalism and Canadian regionalism have been a brake on any such grand political project. Even with Canada's highly centralized executive style of federalism, wherein Ottawa has so much power, Canada never became a neo-liberal copycat of the great Republic. The checks and balances imposed by the Charter on federal-provincial relations have also operated as a partial political firewall against Ottawa's ideological grand vision. And public opposition has acted as an important brake on the government's ambitions. The US has no equivalent, built-in set of institutional restraints. Contemporary American political culture is organized to be a catalyst for non-stop transformation at home, at school, in the workplace and, most of all, in the mass media. With no effective opposition present, families, communities and businesses are required to get with the program. The consequences on the fabric of US society have been equally profound.

As this liberal revolution has gathered steam, equality of opportunity for all, the one standard that Americans had deemed the bedrock of their political system, has been downgraded and downsized. Under the Clinton and Bush presidencies, government no longer has to demonstrate equal concern for every person under its dominion. The idea of treating all people as equals is primarily a legal principle, not a political one. Today the US has some of the most minimal institutional protections for its citizens of any modern community, but paradoxically the American people have more legal rights than any other country in the world.

## Income Security and Economic Integration: Adding Up the Numbers

What continues to make Canada unique and non-American is its institutional mix. It has an "un-American transactional mode of distribution" compared to the US type of market exchange; Canadians look to the state to lower transaction costs, while American voters have not abandoned their preference for the market and the free enterprise system to set things right.[39] The income security gap between the two countries is the most significant difference of all. According to the most authoritative study to date, carried out by two Department of Finance economists, Americans spend 7.1 percent of GDP on income security measures compared to 11 percent for Canada, a massive difference of 3.9 percent[40] (see Table 1). Such measures do the most to reduce income inequality. More than a quarter of Canada's GDP is spent directly or indirectly on redistribution and protecting the social bond.

Canada has done much better than the US in learning to reconcile the efficiency of markets with the values of social community. Canadian national policies have strong redistributive effects, reducing inequality in earnings and diminishing regional disparities. Canada has relied less on income taxes and more on income transfers to contain and reduce inequality. Between 1974 and 1985 the US did a better job in equalizing family incomes, but in the more recent period, because Canada did not dismantle its social welfare system, transfers have had a stronger equalizing effect.

The more generous Canadian programs have made a difference regionally, and for low-income families. The poorest 25 percent of Canadians are better off than their US counterparts, and when Canada's system of transfers is added to market income, the regional impact is often huge. When market income plus transfers are counted together, "one quarter of Canadian families are better off than their US counterparts in terms of purchasing power."[41]

Earnings and income polarization has slowed and moderated

*Table 1. Breakdown of Canada-US Program Spending by Function, 2001 (percent of GDP)*

| Function | US | Canada | Gap |
|---|---|---|---|
| Income security | 7.1 | 11.0 | 3.9 |
| Housing and community services | 0.5 | 1.4 | 0.9 |
| Economic affairs | 3.2 | 3.5 | 0.3 |
| Recreation and culture | 0.3 | 1.0 | 0.7 |
| Education | 6.2 | 5.9 | -0.3 |
| Health | 6.7 | 7.0 | 0.4 |
| General public service | 1.9 | 1.9 | 0.0 |
| Public order and safety | 2.2 | 1.9 | -0.2 |
| National defence | 4.0 | 1.2 | -2.8 |
| Total program spending* | 31.9 | 34.8 | 2.9 |
| Non-defence program spending* | 27.9 | 33.6 | 5.7 |
| Total spending in North America | 27.8 | 31.4 | 3.6 |

*Several adjustments must be made to these figures to reach the national accounts measure of total program spending.

Source: Suzanne Kennedy and Steven Gonzalez, "Government spending in Canada and the US," Department of Finance, Ottawa, Working Paper 2003–05.

across Canada while in the US inequality has sharply increased. Although not all provinces have benefited equally, Ontario and Alberta have moved up, while the four Atlantic provinces remain in the backwaters in terms of income disparity. Even so, leading Statistics Canada experts Wolfson and Murphy's major conclusion is unambiguous. Inequality differences among regions within each country were "smaller than those between the two countries" between 1974 and 1997.[42]

Between 1950 and 1989, Americans expected that their economic situation would improve for each family each year and each decade. Capitalism would be adjusted for democratic ends and inequality kept in check. This was the lynchpin of a US welfare system that has been effectively broken. The earnings of many Americans have stagnated for almost three decades. Between 1974 and 2003, incomes increased about 10 percent, from $32,000 to $36,000. After-tax income for families in the middle of the income pyramid grew by only 10 percent according to the Congressional Budget Office. In the same period, the wealthiest one percent of families saw their incomes rise by 157 percent. The average annual compensation of top CEOs soared from $1.3 million to $37.5 million, an increase of more than one thousand times the pay of ordinary production workers.[43] Today the restructuring of American political life resembles that of the late nineteenth and early twentieth centuries when the state was smaller, private welfare larger and income inequality wider.[44] Legal residents, immigrants and children born in the US but from immigrant families find themselves relegated to the margins of American society, having no access to comprehensive redistributive programs.

## What Do the Causal Arrows Tell Us?

A sociologist might explain the continent's new political geography by saying that North American markets, identity and citizenship were once reinforcing but no longer are. Now two of these three arrows are pointing in sharply opposing directions. Identity and citizenship speak to who we are individually and collectively, and are a matter of positive sovereignty in Canada for promoting the public good. By contrast, economic integration has pushed Canada a long way down the axis of negative sovereignty, limiting public authority's capacity to intervene and protect citizens. Critics correctly argue that North American governments are a shadow of what they once were. They have been left with an outer shell of formal power, an inner skin of neo-liberal beliefs and little political will to act deliberately to promote social and economic justice.[45] But even here the reality on both sides of the border is not the same.

Canadian provinces have not tailored their programs to fit those in US states. The free traders who predicted that the American standard would become the Canadian norm in a matter of years were wrong. Differences within Canada have proven more important than anyone predicted and have slowed down the process of convergence between Canada and the US. Boychuk and Banting, in their detailed examination of policy convergence, conclude that the "overall picture is one of persisting differences.... Core programs continue to evolve along separate pathways."[46]

The picture in North America mirrors the trend across OECD countries. There is no evidence of across-the-board convergence with respect to taxation or public expenditures. In 2003, France and Germany were in violation of the European Union's stability pact by posting deficits of about 3 percent of their gross domestic product. Japan led the pack with a deficit of 7.7 percent, followed by the US at 4.6 percent, a figure predicted to be much higher the next year. Britain's overspending reached 1.9 percent and was rising. Of the Anglo-American countries, Canada was in top place with a putative surplus of 1 percent of GDP in 2003 and the expectation for continued surplus in 2004.[47]

To recognize that Canadian minimum standards are higher than US standards for old age pensions, social assistance, health care and maternity leave is not to note a small difference. No Canadian province has welfare entitlements as low as many US states.[48] In 2002, Canada's child poverty rate was one in six, compared to one in four in the US; 20 percent of Canadians had low-paid employment compared to 25 percent of Americans; private social spending in Canada (4.5 percent) was almost half the US amount (8.6 percent); and employment insurance benefits as a percentage of earnings was 28 percent in Canada but half that level, 14 percent, in the US. Almost 40 percent of Canadian workers were covered by collective bargaining agreements, but only 14 percent of American workers had access to workplace representation.[49]

You are better off receiving social assistance in Ontario than in West Virginia. Even the poorest regions of Canada are better off than the most destitute in the US because of Canada's system of social transfers. Core political and philosophical differences have heightened despite higher levels of economic integration, as North America's two welfare states have been diminished and constrained in very different ways. We can debate the adequacy of Canada's minimum wage, the need for more support to children living in poverty or the thinness of poverty lines, but Canada's level of institutional support sustains a surprisingly resilient and strong domestic social bond.

The temptation is always to adopt policies in favour of the undefended border, but this has never been an adequate framework for a free, diverse and compassionate Canadian society. Only conscious improvement in the institutional framework of Canada and intellectual mastery of the social forces of identity politics can point us in the most desirable direction. Canadians have effectively chosen to limit the kinds of market outcomes that produce "unforeseen results." They are sceptical about the American liberal individualist tradition. Modern Canada's privileging of the collective "we" now constitutes the Great Divide between the north and south of the forty-ninth parallel.

Canadians need to focus a lot more on their own point of view. Canada and the US used to be thought of as similar peoples, but now their dissimilarities with respect to the role of public authority and citizenship obligations have become more visible and compelling. And these divisive trends appear to be increasingly impossible to reverse.

# 4. The Case for Building a North American Community: Is There One?

"La Patrie c'est la terre, et non le sang." —Ringuet, *Trente Arpents* (1938)

## The Search for Consensus

Rising anxiety about the porous Canada-US border has created space for new thinking that is increasingly nation-centred. Integration requires governments to do more, be bolder, take more initiatives and enter into agreements requiring them to act with bounded autonomy. There is also renewed talk about the need for a North American community of some kind, but that option would require more political will and more nation-state power to govern North America effectively. Other experts call for a "North America of regions," to which governments would devolve new powers. The regions would then have greater political responsibility and authority to deliver services and make a difference in the lives of their citizens. It is uncertain how this would work across borders when most states today are cash-strapped and have no resources to deliver existing services. Devolving tax power from the federal level in the US and Canada is probably not possible or desirable.[1]

Politically oriented corporate elites are proposing a deeper integration between the NAFTA partners that would involve new institutions to coordinate social, economic, environmental, fiscal, energy and even cultural policies. This too implies a transfer of power from current institutions to new ones and would depend on both Washington's and Ottawa's willingness to accept a larger role for transnational authority. The transfer of power from the US Congress, Mexico's National Assembly and the Canadian House of Commons would require a dramatic reorganization of democratic life in North America. As Stephen Clarkson has had to admit, after much probing of the new architecture of North America, there is no momentum "towards further consolidation" for broadening or deepening; the much vaunted continental system is "doomed to secondary importance."[2]

None of the futuristic scenarios for a North American community contemplate the end of the nation-state, which has to date been such a dominant feature of the international system.[3] Nor are they any clearer about the future role that citizens would play in the new arrangements. The Great Border cannot be deconstructed, nor can the commercial dimension be taken out of context. Nor is there any reason to take seriously the idea that the US state will suddenly go the way of the plough-horse and support a supranational North America, particularly since Clinton barely mustered enough votes in Congress to pass NAFTA.

The pressing question from a North American perspective is whether the pressures for continent-wide integration will eventually lead to a strengthening of the public interest in many spheres. Such strengthening would entail the provision of new public goods, an intensification of cultural contacts and exchanges between peoples, and the need for a larger role for public authority on both sides of the forty-ninth parallel.

The traditional answer provided by the most rigorous economists is that public services, spaces and places are looked after through public regulation in response to market failure. In the potent words of Jacques Attali, the state and civil society require large, state-constructed "sanctuaries outside market logic," that is, outside the reach of the price system.[4] The necessities of existence have to come from citizens' efforts to enlarge the not-for-profit sector in areas from education through health, to parks and public places. All these public goods, as a responsibility of national authority, enhance the social bond rather than weaken it. It is not by any means clear how they would be supplied in any future arrangement should North American integration be broadened and deepened.

## Expanding the US Side of the Border

So far the social dimension of integration has received little attention, but it ought to. It is a key dimension that must be addressed if there is to be any substance to the belief that a North

American community exists and needs to be brought together. The only certainty is that there is no sign of the border vanishing. It is not apparent how either government could dispense with the border as part of building a North American community. The Bush presidency has definitively addressed this matter in a spate of new legislative initiatives. Homeland security has made the border an integral part of US domestic policy, making any discussion about deepening and broadening largely academic. Security matters divide the continent along an east-west axis and the border has become more omnipresent, not less. With so many competing agendas, does the big idea of a North American community have a bright future? Or is it just another policy initiative that will never make it out of the pack?

## In Search of North America

Since the idea emerged in the 1920s, historians and other experts have been searching for the existence of "the North American community" with a lot of conviction but little success. How are we to establish a viable belief in North America as a social entity when we do not share the same history, linguistic heritage or culture? What would be the proper role for the state? Is it to enhance the efficiency of markets? Or is it to protect the public from rent-seeking private actors? The idea that there is a North American community waiting to emerge is premature and almost surreal, as we have yet to define what that would be, let alone how to strengthen and broaden it.

There is no consensus about these and other critical issues, such as the place of the border in bringing the continent closer together. If there were, it would be simpler to speak about the North American community not in the singular but in the plural and see it taking shape locally, regionally and nationally in Canada, Mexico and the US. Frankly, looking across the continent, it is difficult to see any civic-minded agency capable of building community and developing the social dimension in North America.

## A Big Idea without Policy Legs

If the case for building the North American community is to have any legs, institutions will be critical in developing the policy environment. The key institution in any deepening is NAFTA, but

NAFTA has no effective executive, no legislative function and no mandate for reform and it is ill-equipped to be a brake on US sovereignty. NAFTA does have a very powerful but flawed disputes-settlement mechanism to address complex social and environmental issues. Indeed, the number of trade disputes has grown post-NAFTA rather than diminished, but NAFTA has not curbed US protectionist pressures in the least. This is the principal reason why the Bush administration favours the status quo and is opposed to any attempt to develop a stronger trade regime, or what experts call "deep integration." North American integration does not need to take the proverbial next step. The "commercial club model" is fully operational, relying on the US appetite for energy, agricultural imports, cheaply produced goods from the maquiladoras and the North American auto industry. Measured in terms of annual growth in exports, the conventional standard (not mine), NAFTA is a success story.

Three-way trade has doubled since 1994, the year of its implementation, reaching $660 billion annually. The figures are dizzying to contemplate. Trade between Canada and the US averages $1.2 billion per day and US–Mexico trade has soared to $720 million daily.[5] From a trade-theory perspective, probably as much as 50 percent of the trade is intra-firm and not a NAFTA effect, but these new economic linkages have become a principal selling point for the next phase. Cross-border investment now binds Canada and Mexico to US financial markets so closely that the belief is we are already on the way to building a North American community. The next stage is to break down the barriers that supposedly continue to distort investment and trade and drive up costs to consumers.

There is an "Alice in Wonderland" naivety to this recycled vision of the free trade debates. Perrin Beatty, the president of Canadian Manufacturers and Exporters has asserted, without any factual basis, that it is easier for "Canadian business to sell in the US than between Canadian provinces."[6] Hardly, according to John Helliwell, who states that, "The typical Canadian province trades 12 times as much in goods with another Canadian province as with a US state of similar size and distance. For services, the 'home bias' is 2 to 3 times stronger than for goods."[7] Even so, the central question remains: Is NAFTA flexible enough to establish

North America as a social entity and not simply a market opportunity?

## A Decade of Free Trade: Uncertainty and Instability

A decade of integration has produced many changes in North America. Powerful corporate interests have hollowed out state authority, leaving it with a hard outer shell of formal power but less interest to act aggressively to redistribute income. Cutbacks and reduced state spending on social programs have reduced the public sphere and the redistributive supply of collective goods. To build a North American community, Canadians and Americans will have to strike a new balance between the border's multiple functions—as an identity line, security barrier, high-profile regulatory fence and commercial swing gate. Finding this equilibrium point has been elusive for policy elites.

NAFTA's commitment to across-the-board commercial flexibility marked a new departure for public policy and established a dangerous precedent for the future. It has worked against deepening the social dimension of North America and accentuated national diversity (see Table 2). In Mexico, for instance, a country with 40 percent poverty rates, real wages are the most significant indicator of economic progress, and they fluctuated widely over the 1990s. In fact, Mexico's GDP growth, current account balance and inflation have all fluctuated tremendously since it became a NAFTA member, and Mexico's growth path has become more unstable. Mexico did better prior to NAFTA with a growth in real wages of 6.6 and 8.9 percent in 1991 and 1992. The figures for the NAFTA decade are poor and largely negative: 3.7 percent in 1994, -13.5 percent in 1995, -11.1 percent in 1996, -0.6 percent in 1997 and then very small gains, 2.2 percent in 1998 and 1.4 percent in 1999.[8]

In hindsight, the expectation that Mexico's market gains would pay off in the space of one or two years was wildly unrealistic. Lustig calculates that the 1994 peso crisis cost Mexico one million jobs and its average wages declined by 13.5 percent.[9] Over the next three years, real wages in manufacturing fell by some 30 percent, creating new advantages for US investors. Poverty rose by almost 20 percent following the crisis, as Mexico lacked the mechanisms and means to help poor people devas-

Table 2. NAFTA at a Glance, 1999

| | GDP (% of NAFTA total) | Population (%) | Trade Dependency on NAFTA Markets (% of goods exported) | Inequality (ratio of income, top 10% of population to bottom 10%), for 2000 |
|---|---|---|---|---|
| United States | 90 | 69 | 36 | 16.6 |
| Canada | 6 | 7 | 86 | 8.5 |
| Mexico | 4 | 24 | 86 | 32.6 |
| Total (millions) | $9,795,870 | 409 | $1,068,110 | |

Source: Wendy Dobson, "Shaping the Future of North American Economic Space," C.D. Howe Institute, 2002, p. 6; Jim Stanford, "The North American Free Trade Agreement: Context, Structure, and Performance," in Jonathan Michie, ed., *The Handbook of Globalisation* (London: University of London, 2003).

tated by this external shock. Other studies have found that public spending for the poor contracted more than any other non-debt-related spending.[10]

With North America's policy environment skewed to the integration end of the spectrum, there is no new day for Mexico's poor and few prospects to build on in the future. It is wrong-headed to believe that Mexico will grow out of poverty or that North America shares a common future simply because exports are soaring. Lustig estimates that if Mexico's economy grew persistently at five percent a year, it would take almost fifty years for high growth rates to eradicate extreme poverty as defined by the proportion of the population living on $2 a day. By comparison, a 2 percent transfer of income from the top decile (0.90 percent of GDP) to households and persons living at the bottom of the economic order would eradicate poverty.[11] No amount of incremental market access through NAFTA is going to resolve this challenge for Mexico or for those living beneath the poverty line throughout North America. We are not coming together as a continent, and unequal border effects are major points of public policy contention.

## Predictions So Wide of the Mark

Economic integration has not transformed North America into a solid and cohesive trade bloc with an ability to grow in response to civil society's needs and demands. Attempts to establish the case for a broader and larger policy framework for North America by enlisting the support of macroeconomic models remains highly suspect. Faith-based models that forecast only positive outcomes from free trade are intellectual abstractions from the real world, not evidence driven. Think of it this way. In one corner is the perfect free trade theory and in the other are the outcomes. The two do not match at all. We need to stop and reflect on why the predictions were so wide of the mark.

The original theoretical work in support of continental free trade promised millions of new jobs for North Americans, higher growth rates, a superior standard of living and real per capita income gains, but these did not materialize. The idea that convergence would be automatic proved incorrect. Contrary to expectations, overall NAFTA gains have been insignificant for the US, very small for Canada and extremely disruptive for Mexico. Canada's competitive dollar, the devalued peso and the US asset boom, driven by high-tech stocks and new technologies, have been more critical for export success than any other single group of factors. In the US, the collapse of collective bargaining in many sectors and the low minimum wage have had a more detrimental impact on US wages than all of the job losses from low-wage Mexican competition.

In one empirical study, Hinojosa et al. found that, given the size of the US economy, job losses were modest at best. Between 1990 and 1997, the growth of Mexican imports caused an overall loss of 300,000 jobs, or an average of 37,000 per year. Given that the US economy was creating over 200,000 jobs per month, the direct NAFTA effect was insignificant.[12] By comparison, aggregate changes in the US trade deficit were so massive that they swamped the job losses caused by changes in bilateral trade between the NAFTA partners.

For most of the NAFTA decade, the US employment level has been determined principally by the Federal Reserve and its interest rate policy. Any future benefits from deep integration will encounter similar limitations. US corporations have many other strategic markets that compete with NAFTA's. US-NAFTA trade accounts for less than a third of total US trade. In fact, US trade with other partners has become more important and grown more quickly. In 1996, total US trade in merchandise stood at $1.4 trillion and by 2000 it was just under $2 trillion, a 42 percent increase. By comparison, NAFTA trade grew from just under $1 billion to $1.3 billion, a 30 percent climb. US trade with the rest of the world overwhelms trade with its two NAFTA partners.[13]

With the Canadian and American inflation rates close to zero and Mexico's rate at historically low levels, there is little evidence that governments have turned their attention to the primary role of supporting human development goals for their citizens. The redistributive effort of all three governments, as measured by total spending on programs devoted to social improvement and investment in human capital, is less than it was a decade ago. Canada remains a high spender despite a decade of dis-investment in all kinds of redistributive programs. Social spending amounts to approximately 31 percent of GDP and appears to be on the rise again. The baseline figure for the US is roughly 27 percent of GDP, and spending is declining for many programs. Congress is demanding that more of its health and social security programs be privatized to reduce costs. It wants to impose new laws that will require federal departments to compete with the private sector to deliver services. None of this provides reassuring evidence that the government is thinking about rebuilding programs devastated by cutbacks.

For Mexico, the benchmark measure for social spending is about half the US figure and probably less. President Vicente Fox has failed to invest significantly in education and health reforms. In the words of Isidro Morales, one of Mexico's sharpest NAFTA's analysts, "economic and social fragmentation is on the way, creating new pressure on state bureaucracies."[14]

What is missing in North America is a commitment from all three governments to maintain social cohesion, strengthen the redistributive role of government and enforce sound governance principles as defined by United Nations Human Development Report. This would require more state and less market, and even this proposition is unlikely to be adopted. The collective mind of North America is too materialistic, too complacent and too consumed by novelty to imagine a strategic view of NAFTA's potentiality. Being North Americans, our "thoughts and imaginings," to use the evocative words of George Grant, are much more likely to support a mixture of public order and individualism than any collective supranational project.[15]

## Active Localisms against Supranational North America

Since the battle in Seattle in 1999 and the Quebec Summit in 2001, strong active localisms have raised awareness that the border and border effects are more important than ever, despite globalization and the belief that borders matter less. Regulatory diversity has led to new controversies about the relationship between trade and domestic sovereignty with respect to health and labour standards, trade unionism, and trade and investment. Many US states have reduced their labour standards and restricted the right of unions to organize, while in Quebec, workplace standards have been tightened and Canada-wide collective bargaining covers almost 40 percent of the work force.[16] Examples such as these underline the fact that constraints and policy differences have grown more visible as many non-trade policy issues now operate as a continental fault line between the three NAFTA countries. This is evidence that institutions, as products of social interaction, and not simply elites or markets, are critical to maintaining the values and practices that society requires to protect the social bond.[17]

In North America the emphasis—to borrow Michael Trebilcock's critical distinction—has been on negative integration.[18] Negative integration sets out the rules of what countries cannot do and is largely responsible for the "less state, less tax" policy harmonization process that has led to spending cuts everywhere. By contrast, positive integration would spell out the supranational regulatory rules and the domestic policy standards that the US, Mexico and Canada *must* adopt. Without positive integration there is no trinational framework to protect social standards and strengthen social inclusion. There is no built-in escalator that requires all three countries to spend more on social North America and invest in human capital. In fact, under market fundamentalist principles, program spending has been cut to meet artificially imposed deficit reduction targets. Nor does this framework provide incentives to increase health and labour standards. Not unexpectedly, negative integration provides the US with the legal clout to impose its will on its weaker partners. As a result, positive integration remains on permanent hold, and access to the US market for Canada and Mexico remains contingent, limited, unpredictable and subject to US trade law and the trade politics of the US Congress.

## Too Many "Thou Shalt Nots": Privileging US Interests

These structural and policy constraints are dampening any dynamic for a further phase of North American integration. The principal stumbling block remains the negative model of integration embodied in NAFTA that presents state/market relations as a series of "thou shalt nots" rather than regulatory "shoulds." Practically speaking, the national economic space behind the border is shrinking and the ducks are not lining up to bring the continent closer together. There are many obstacles in the way of deepening the North American community and a number have their origins in NAFTA's legal and economic framework. The principal one is that NAFTA is a commercial agreement and cannot address the social effects of integration. Freer markets have not generated better services, and the policy environment is increasingly sceptical about further economic integration that does not address the social dimension.

One of the most important obstacles to political and social integration is the very large "home bias effect," the way the US Congress privileges US interests and, as a result, American corporations have derived the largest share of the benefits from economic integration. Paradoxically, giving US corporations privileged access to the continental market undermines support for a larger agenda of political integration.

This bias can also be found nestled amongst many rules in the NAFTA agreement, including rules of origin, national presence and national treatment, and in the legal culture that prevents Mexico and Canada from using national presence and national treatment for developmental or regional programs. Legislators must think twice whether new programs may potentially run afoul of NAFTA rules, which are themselves not definitive but in need of interpretation. Since they are subject to legal challenge from US lobbyists and industries, public policymakers face a great deal of uncertainty and risk.[19]

The US Congress has disregarded NAFTA's rules in the case of softwood lumber, unilaterally imposing punishing tariffs on Canadian producers. Canada has filed three disputes at the WTO and three before NAFTA panels, challenging US protectionist practices. There is no guarantee of congressional compliance. The US Congress will decide whether or not to end its illegal practices, and if it appears that the WTO or NAFTA decision will go against it, it will try to force Canada to accept a settlement that protects its wrongdoing. The most likely scenario is that Canada will compromise its legal rights, impose an export tax and limit its share of the US market. For government pragmatists NAFTA is only a bargaining chip, not an inviolate high standard.

And in a move that bears many similarities to the softwood lumber situation, the US Congress has also tried to rewrite the rules with respect to Mexico's sugar exports. From a US perspective, as long as Mexico was a net importer of US sugar, the playing field was level. But the US sugar lobby viewed the NAFTA agreement as being too generous and opposed any attempt by Mexico to reduce the quantity of US imports flooding the Mexican market. Basically, the US wants to ship unlimited quantities of sugar to Mexico while reducing Mexico's sugar exports to the US.[20] There has been no resolution to this major, ongoing trade dispute in the past seven years. It is significant that Washington bears no legal or political costs for non-compliance on softwood lumber or sugar.

In another instance, the US Congress passed legislation that prevents Mexican truckers from using US highways until the drivers have been certified for safety regulations and are competent and proficient in English. At present, Mexican truckers are not allowed more than twenty miles beyond the US border, where they are required to transfer their loads to US companies. This system guarantees US transportation companies a lucrative national market free from competition with Mexican transporters.

Technically, Mexican transporters have market access, but the rules have been set aside as both the Clinton and Bush administrations have capitulated to a coalition of the Teamsters union and environmentalists. Almost a decade of experience in many areas reveals that NAFTA's obligations do not override US congressional authority.[21] The US Commerce Secretary tried to break the impasse by giving Mexican truckers the green light to operate in the US. He had to go over the head of Congress to get NAFTA rules enforced. But the Teamsters appealed successfully to a San Francisco court, which overruled the US Commerce Secretary on the grounds that he did not have the power to "weaken safety standards" that protect the environment. Mexico has had to confront the fact that, as a practical matter, NAFTA's legal guarantees are not always binding. Although the NAFTA text guarantees Mexico access, a US court can overrule the agreement when challenged. This is but one more example of the "home bias effect" that tilts the playing field in favour of the US.

NAFTA's legal provisions have not constrained protectionist forces in the US Congress, which operate legally and without fear of reprisal or penalty from any transnational authority. US trade politics have shown themselves immune to many of NAFTA's legal rules and practices. Recently, a San Diego court ruled against the Department of Energy, which had granted building permits for cross-border power stations to help relieve California's energy crisis.[22] On this occasion, environmentalists opposed the construction of these sites and stopped the project from proceeding. The larger issue here is that when there is a conflict between NAFTA trade law and US law and administrative practice, US law prevails. American interests are institutionally privileged while Canadians and Mexicans find themselves outsiders in the US political and legislative system. Even when Washington is in conformity with NAFTA's codes, it hides behind its own legal rules, administrative procedures and power politics to gain tactical advantage.

## Legal Access: No Guarantee against a Protectionist Congress

The possibility of a new architecture emerging for North America is seriously compromised by NAFTA's invasive legal culture, which makes the deeper integration necessary for new state-to-state cooperation next to impossible. For instance, both Canada and Mexico are interdicted from using national presence and national treatment for developmental ends. This can only be interpreted as a kind of reverse discrimination that advantages US interests. Giving private investors national treatment status to invest and divest without public oversight is the wrong regulatory response to economic integration. This is a classic instance of negative integration—a "thou shalt not."

Under the existing legal regime, Canada has the right to design a regulatory public interest framework provided that it does not run afoul of NAFTA's stringent first principles.[23] Of course, any new public interest regulation must not discriminate against US investment rights or any other part of the legal framework. A priori, no government department knows exactly where the line needs to be drawn and whether its proposed legislation crosses it. From a policy point of view, trade agreements have many "perverse effects" arising from the unpredictability of the policy environment. These in turn limit the capacity of government to be innovative. Both the Clinton and Bush governments have opposed Mexican and Canadian requests to revisit the critical issue of investment rights.

Under NAFTA's Chapter 11, corporations have the right to sue democratically elected governments for current and future business losses when these powerful actors judge that their return on investment has been compromised by government policy. Investors do not have to go through their own government but are able to trigger a dispute independently if any of the NAFTA's investment rules are breached. The chapter is very general and couched in broad terms. Transnational corporations (TNCs) are given special standing to make public policy.

NAFTA is welcomed by business interests as a multi-level governance structure that can be deployed to weaken the specific authority of national bureaucracies. It devolves power away from democratic authority to non-elected, administrative and commercial tribunals. In the words of Sun Belt's president, a NAFTA complainant, "because of NAFTA, we are now stakeholders in the national water policy of Canada."[24] These are dangerous and difficult powers to constrain.

## Chapter 11's Win-Loss Record

So far, twenty-five cases have been filed under Chapter 11. The win-loss rate varies, since some cases were withdrawn and appeals are pending in others, but after a decade of experience, corporations win better than 40 percent of the time. The amount of money at stake is staggering. By 2003, multinational corporations (MMCs) had claimed $12.55 billion (US) in damages against Canada, $2.6 billion against the US and $501 million against Mexico. Settlements are dramatically less, but the chilling effects far exceed the millions of dollars paid out in damages.[25] The number of cases filed under NAFTA's dispute mechanism is much higher when only final outcomes are counted. While Chapter 11 does not directly challenge national tribunals, it does provide corporations with a powerful legal weapon that can be used offensively against all three governments. The most grievous flaw is that Chapter 11 does not hold corporations criminally responsible for actions that are harmful to others. There is no provision to make transnational corporate actors legally accountable when they operate across jurisdictions.

The right to sue a government in the exercise of its democratically elected duties is a very aggressive measure. NAFTA's Chapter 11 provides corporations with rights that previously no trade agreement had granted to business interests.[26] Commercial disputes cover many issues including contract violation, non-performance requirements, copyright infringement and the like. Since the late forties, under international law, companies have had legal recourse against expropriation without compensation, though not as an absolute right. In practice, when a corporation's assets and operations were nationalized, the investors' home government would try to obtain compensation by political means, negotiating with the government to reach a settlement. According to the most authoritative study, few corporations came away empty-handed.[27] NAFTA changed the balance of power in this critical area, creating a new asymmetry. Multinational corporations are entitled to demand compensation as a legal right when, in their view, they are denied "fair and equitable treatment" by any of the three governments.

## North America's Public Interest at Risk

In the case of *Ethyl Corporation v. Canada,* Ottawa was sued for banning MMT, a dangerous chemical additive to gasoline, and in *S.D. Myers v. Canada,* the Canadian government was again sued for banning the export of PCB waste to the United States. Canadian authorities were also sued by UPS. The courier company argued that Canada Post used its public monopoly to reduce the costs of its commercial services. The B.C. provincial and Canadian federal governments were sued by the California-based Sun Belt Inc. for their refusal to consent to the export of bulk water. Public authorities in Mexico and the US have also been subject to litigation in the area of public health and the environment (*Methanex Corporation v. United States of America* and *Metalclad v. The United Mexican States*). In these critical, trend-setting disputes, corporations have won five out of six decisions. Each settlement has had direct public policy implications and resulted in lower standards, reversed public interest legislation or negatively affected the delivery of public services.[28]

The source of this attack on the North American public domain is traceable to the way that Chapter 11 defines a "protectable investment" so broadly that it includes almost any kind of business activity. It could be a business interest arising from a financial commitment, to a policy related to human resources, or any other kind of legitimate economic activity that runs afoul of NAFTA's rules. Expropriation is another concept so loosely defined as to include any government measure that restricts investment rights even when the government is acting to protect the public interest in matters of health or the environment. Expropriation includes not only the more traditional notion of nationalization, but also any measures that are tantamount to indirect expropriation as well.[29] The open-ended nature of Chapter 11 and the lack of strict definitions has been an incentive for MNCs to invoke it in ways that the trade negotiators never envisaged.

## Comparing NAFTA Rules to Other Legal Regimes: Are They up to Standard?

Compared to other legal regimes such as human rights legislation, anti-trust legislation or competition policy, NAFTA trade law is less stringent. It provides no requirement that the public interest be protected.

Why should trade law have such lower standards than these other legal regimes? The authoritative answer is that because trade law is designed expressly to protect business interests, it does not have to take into account public interest or civil society's needs.

Whether advertently or not, trade law compromises the public interest by prioritizing the private over the public.

For instance, under NAFTA rules, no multinational corporation could be found guilty of illegally maintaining a monopoly as Microsoft was under US anti-trust legislation. The subsequent settlement between the US Department of Justice and nine US states was criticized as being too soft on Microsoft. A commercial agreement should have the capacity to address monopolistic practices, but nothing like this exists in NAFTA. In the US, the regulation of investment and corporate practices requires constant oversight through the Securities and Exchange Commission. Financial institutions are monitored, investigated and punished when they break the law. NAFTA has no capacity to protect the public interest and prosecute wrongdoing.

With the Enron and other corporate "insider" scandals over the last few years, corporate governance is a front-burner issue. New, tougher regulations are being proposed for the financial industry and the telecom market. NAFTA is now out of step as a legal instrument, because it has no capacity to punish corporate law-breaking. To shed its powerful corporate bias, North American integration requires a powerful and independent legal authority to ensure that the corporations follow the rules and are held accountable for their actions. The competition directorate of the European Union (EU) is a powerful agency with the legal authority to subpoena, seize documents, undo takeovers and prosecute firms and governments that fail to comply with its orders. Many experts are of the view that its regulatory powers are inadequate. Competitive markets cannot function without regulatory oversight, and in North America each NAFTA partner has its "domestic competition police" to prosecute powerful corporate actors when they break the law. Critically, there is no NAFTA authority charged with this crucial responsibility.

Broadening and deepening integration in North America requires innovative and strong national public interest legislation, not new trade litigation measures. The regulatory fence at the border requires strengthening and enforcement to protect communities on both sides. So far, Chapter 11 provisions have trumped any attempt to hold corporations accountable and protect North America's diverse communities.

## Defining North America as a Community

According to Robert Bellah, a community is a group of people who are socially interdependent, who share and participate in decision-making, share common political and social practices and are open to new experiences.[30] The latter point is crucial because a North American community cannot be said to exist until key sections of public opinion decide, through deliberate effort, to have common institutions that reflect vital shared experiences.

At its core, community is place-bound and socially directed, and requires positive regulation to ensure the distribution of collective and public goods. A community must make political choices, establish priorities and act collectively. It requires civically dedicated institutions with "paramount legislative authority," to use Michael Trebilcock's well-chosen phrase.

By contrast, markets work optimally through negative regulatory competition policies; they are about individual opportunity and the protection of private interest. Markets respect no border and undermine the territorial "thereness" of place, challenging the political authority of democratically constituted states. Market-driven integration, using trade as a crow bar to promote convergence or harmonization as an end in itself, cannot respect the preference of citizens to choose the standards they desire.

Democratic institutions arise out of social interaction backed by democratic rule. They require a strong and vibrant notion of the public interest. So, any deepening and broadening of NAFTA that does not require the dominant power to cede and pool sovereignty is proceeding with the wrong agenda. This will not promote regulatory diversity as a primary framework to strengthen public authority and address common transnational problems, from poverty eradication to energy conservation.

At the present time the North American commons is in danger from powerful, private, rent-seeking actors. Economic geographers have long insisted that the new North America is defined by the mega-energy projects that run underground or overhead. Neither people nor communities are part of this equation. These causeways of commerce and energy flows are vast conduits that have broken all records. Canada's resource-based exports doubled from $40 billion in 1989 to almost $90 billion in 1998. In 1998, Canada pumped more than $25 billion in oil and gas to US markets, growing at a dizzying pace of more than 10 percent per year.[31] Presently they constitute an empire of one-way streets of energy and electricity shipments from the Canadian north to the US south, southwest and northeast.

The corporations are no longer familiar household names like Canadian Pacific or Canadian National, but are top-heavy energy giants, such as Canada Transmission Mainline, Transcontinental, Trailblazer, CNG, Transwestern, PGT and PG&E, which carry billions of cubic metres of gas to the American markets. Oil pipelines also traverse the continent, linking Montreal to Chicago and points south. Feeder lines move Canada's black gold from Alberta and Saskatchewan into the American southwest. American energy enterprises have shown no special power for taking from the have regions to provide for the have-nots on a transcontinental basis. Quite the contrary. The mega-investment flows of the past decade have not served as a launching pad from which to knit the regions of North American into a more coherent economic entity; rather, they protect the interests of the American consumer behind the border with a secure and cheap supply of Canadian energy. They have enlisted the public energy utilities of Ontario, Quebec, New Brunswick and Manitoba—all cash-starved provinces—to join this energy export drive on a continental basis.[32]

With NAFTA rules privileging corporate interests, citizens in Canada and Mexico are looking inwards, rather than south or north, for more public and collective goods and to meet the new challenges. They are searching for ways to strengthen their national space, not to extend it beyond the border.

## North America's Culture of Active Localisms with a Strong National Bent

So far, our loyalties and identities remain significantly nation-centred. North America's nation-states "not only reign, but rule," and continue to be obeyed and honoured in almost all of the high political domains.[33] They continue to be powerful entities. There is no sign of an eclipse of the nation state, but there are trickle-down effects that constrain state policy. If present-day history is any guide, North Americans are first and foremost active localists with a strong national bent. If we are born in Vancouver, attend a university in Toronto and then choose to live in Montreal, we will have different identities at different times in our lives. The old idea that we all have a singular regional identity is quite wrong.[34]

North America has always allowed its inhabitants to change their local identities for different durations, and hence our social diversity is rooted so profoundly in omnipresent national flavours and markings. For a part of one's life, one may be a New Yorker, then a Californian and then a Texan. North American integration has not degraded the border with respect to our micro-identities. Mobility is strongly east-west within Canada and even more so within the Republic to the south. Few Texans migrate to Canada, but many Ontarians head west and become instant Albertans, with anti-Ottawa views to match. Our regional identities are overwhelmingly national, not continental. Canada's south has nothing geographically in common with the US south. Documented cross-border institutional connections between communities and regions are weak and underdeveloped.[35]

No American community has adopted Canadian social standards of employment, health or education. In terms of values, Canada and the US are on divergent paths, as Michael Adams has so powerfully demonstrated. A decade ago, 42 percent of Americans agreed that the father was the master of his family and, in 2000, 49 percent supported this proposition. In Canada, support for the traditional notion that "father knows best" fell to 18 percent from close to 25 percent a decade earlier.[36] Certainly Canada is no longer the conservative, hide-bound society that it once was. We have embraced the civic republican values of equity and openness. The US, once strongly egalitarian and populist, has become deeply socially conservative. Borderlines are real markers for everyone but economists with their abstract models.

Where there is a strong North American presence is in the cosmopolitan cities of the continent, including Toronto, Montreal, Vancouver, New York, Los Angeles and Chicago. These mega-cities are home to multicultural populations. Los Angles has 200,000 Canadians and hundreds of thousands of Mexicans. There are over 100,000 former draft dodgers living in the greater Toronto area and about 400,000 South Asians call the region home. The universal ordinals on the compass point north, south, east and west, but what do they really tell us that is not country-bound and place specific?

## The Future of North America as a Social Entity

North America's public policymakers face a tough dilemma: they can be fixers and try to shrink NAFTA, making it less intrusive than it is; they can increase its reach and try to find ways to make it binding on the US; or they can try to negotiate a NAFTA-plus agreement that would require a larger role for the market. So far there is no compelling case for taking any of these next steps. North America requires innovative and strong national public interest legislation, not a new trade deal. "North Americans," in the collective sense of the term, need to put their national economies in order and find ways to address the actual problems of poverty, regional inequality, immigration and the under-supply of public goods and services. They need to rebuild their national institutions before tackling something infinitely more complex.

If we want to establish North America as a social entity, it must engage the citizens of all three countries and not simply policy and trade elites. More and better information has to be made available and even more than this, the process has to be transparent and democratically accountable. Without substantive participation from civil society and social movements, North American integration is unlikely to proceed towards a social redefinition of North America.[37] There is no "there" there for civil society.

With close to a hundred states and provinces, hundreds of regulatory authorities, three governments, four territories and more than twenty thousand municipalities, there is no North American community waiting to emerge. We used to think that as countries entered the post-national era, borders and border management would be relegated to the back burner. Not so. The corrosive impact of economic globalization has barely broken the powerful hold of territory over collective identity. Even though the sovereignty of the border is not about to fade away, powerful public and private entities in the US and Canada remain intent on changing our fundamental preoccupation with territoriality and identity.

The integration process has been anything but smooth, and the internal dynamics have been difficult to manage. Trade dynamics are not like a 1-800 number or a user-friendly virtual reality. Structural obstacles to further broadening and deepening have increased, and there are many points of systemic friction. All of these developments bring us back to the importance of borders and the future of North America. What have we learned, if anything?

# 5. THE SECURITY-FIRST BORDER: A NORTH AMERICAN QUANDARY

> "In terms of ideas, anything is possible—what is needed is a master hypothesis." —Jean Baudrillard, from *Impossible Exchange*

## The End of the Undefended Border and Continental Destiny

Post–September 11, the border is expected to operate like a Kevlar vest, stopping everything in its path, without hindering the free movement of goods and services. What an abrupt turnaround from an age of free trade when openness was everything and security only a secondary consideration. Of course, it can't be both, a security-tight border and a border geared for commerce with minimum restrictions at the same time. Eventually one must dominate the other. (See Figure 2.) Ottawa has yet to absorb the fact that the commerce-first border that every business leader worked so hard to achieve is yesterday's story. The dilemma is that Americans also don't want a super-tight border. They don't want to be body-searched and, most emphatically, corporate USA doesn't want its Canadian production facilities to face delays when shipping goods back and forth across the border. It is in their interest to trade, and the US will do business wherever it can for oil, manufactured goods and services of every variety.

Canada's economic elites are not good readers of the mood of the US Congress. In an address to Canadian chief executives in Washington, James Carville, a former presidential advisor, described the fallout from Ottawa's decision not to send troops to Iraq as a "pothole." No one in Washington talks about retaliation. Canada's business leaders are gripped by a non-existent problem. Tom D'Acquino, head of the Canadian Council of Chief Executives, finally admitted that cross-border ties have not deteriorated,

*Figure 2. The Security First Border After 9/11*

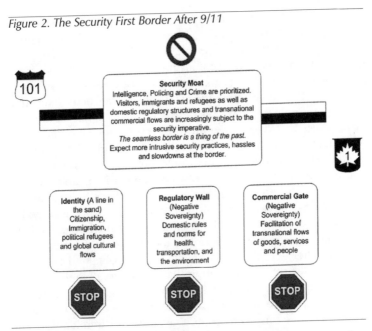

and was forced to retreat from his earlier warnings about the dire consequences facing Canadian exporters from Ottawa's decision not to back the Bush invasion of Iraq.[1]

US corporate heads have not pushed alarm buttons about the border closing down. They have not panicked the way corporate Canada has, and North American commerce has certainly not been endangered by the US security-first doctrine. The current priority of the Bush administration is to address long-term relations with its most important allies, as these require a lot of fixing because of the Iraqi war. Canada appears a long way down the list after France, Germany, Russia, Turkey, Mexico, Brazil and China.

## The Post-9/11 Security-First Border

Many things look different for Canada in this security-obsessed age of strategy, might and law. The Homeland Security Act of 2002,[2] the Public Health and Bio-terrorism Preparedness Response Act of 2002[3] and the Patriot Act of 2001 have placed management of the Canada-US border directly under congressional and executive authority in ways that are unprecedented. These and other measures authorize police and intelligence authorities to expand electronic surveillance and detain and remove aliens suspected of engaging in "terrorist activity."

These landmark bills grant sweeping powers to law enforcement agencies and increase the extralegal powers of the executive arm of government by means of executive and other administrative orders that do not require public hearings or obligate the president to ask Congress for additional authority. They rely on secret warrants or compulsory disclosures that expand the capability of the Justice Department to obtain warrants and conduct searches without publicly disclosing them immediately. Among other things, the new laws allow Internet monitoring, give police access to business records that include library and bookstore files, and authorize emergency searches and electronic surveillance. In the year after 9/11 the Department of Justice obtained 113 secret emergency search authorizations, compared to 47 in the twenty-three years prior to the attack.[4] More than eight million FBI files were provided to the State Department and 85,000 records of suspected persons were turned over to the Immigration and Naturalization Service. These expanded powers of the central security state would seem to violate the Fourth Amendment's protection against "unreasonable searches and seizures."

September 11 redefined not only the border but also North America as a geopolitical region. So far Ottawa remains uncertain as to how it should define itself on the US perimeter. It can play a symbolic "filler" role in the war against terrorism. When intervention requires a military presence, experts reckon that Canada can send up to 2,500 soldiers, although even that modest contribution stretches Canada's military to the limit. From a military point of view, Canada has little to offer the US war machine.

With the Canada-US relationship no longer open-ended, more than ever Canada must acquire a strategic culture for the twenty-first century. The transformed border as security moat, regulatory fence, identity line in the sand and commercial opportunity lies at the centre of this decision. Canada has to become assertive about its side of the border. As a first priority it must conduct a full-scale audit of the US Homeland Security and

Patriot Acts to determine their impact on Canadian public policy and their cross-border effects. So far, no public hearings have been scheduled on this task. The Canadian government is handicapped because it has not consulted across government or with provinces about US homeland security and its extraterritorial consequences for immigration, refugee policy, intelligence, commerce and public regulation. The scope and speed of US legislative and legal change is dramatic and unprecedented in recent times, and the Canadian public has not been kept fully informed.

By 2005 or 2006, it is expected that US border practices will have changed beyond recognition from what they were in 2003. Many of these changes will not simply focus on the US border but on the processes behind and beyond the border. The globalization of US domestic policy is driven by a singular aim: to secure the future of "our nation," "American democracy" and "border security" anywhere Washington believes it is threatened.[5] It will decide what the "security danger" is and how it should be "neutralized." The choices for Canada are stark—to be a tactical sceptic or a trusting loyalist. Either way the answer to this fundamental issue has to be found in Canada, not Washington.[6] Ottawa has not thought through its strategic response to maximize its foreign policy assets. Belatedly it still needs to.

## Asymmetry, Political Will and Destiny

For the United States the northern border with Canada has historically been low maintenance. For much of the twentieth century, State Department officials saw no reason to have a Canadian desk for addressing relations with Canada in a systematic fashion. In Washington's eyes the US-Canada relationship fell into a grey zone, neither totally foreign nor domestic; it belonged somewhere in between.

Canada was assumed to be part of the US homeland perimeter in North America for American security, energy and investment purposes. Canadian anxieties around sovereignty required that it be treated as a separate country for commerce, social policy, migration and trade. Integration accelerated the separation between the political and economic realms. This uncoupling has left Canada more exposed to Washington's aggressive unilateralism in setting North America's agenda post–September 11. The American notion of national security is US-centred and requires only limited cooperation from Canada in tightening, monitoring and implementing its border security practices.

## The Bush Security Doctrine and Diplomacy: The US Shield of the Twenty-first Century

The Bush security doctrine was inspired in no small way by George Schultz, Secretary of State in the early 1980s. Schultz framed the fundamentals of US foreign policy in terms of realism and preparedness. National security required in-depth strategic analyses of all locations where US interests were threatened. Military force would be used pre-emptively to attack any nation judged to pose a significant threat. The overwhelming military power of the US afforded it the means to enforce this agenda. The readiness of US forces to respond globally to all threats, including regime change, reflected the new moral certitude of the US administration. It is only in the final instance that diplomacy and coalition-building is relied upon in the pursuit of this unilateral agenda. US policy is being driven by the real and symbolic significance of the border as a forbidding security moat.

The task of developing cooperative practices in an international environment that is increasingly unstable and unpredictable requires, according to the Schultz canon, the ability to make threat-based assessments backed up by military might. Diplomacy by conventional means is secondary. From the US homeland security perspective, the old distinctions between foreign and domestic, or between state and territory do not hold as they did during the Cold War. The operative principle of "for the good of wider security" requires that the US expand its military presence around the globe in numbers unseen since the Cold War. The expanded military footprint has begun both at home and in other countries as far-flung as the Philippines, Brazil, Uruguay, Argentina, Colombia, Bosnia and Kosovo—all have US special forces or regular troops stationed there.

At the same time, the US has embarked on establishing, with its own citizens and closest collaborators, an enforceable constitutional order of rules and strategic interests anchored in US law and homeland security.[7] The common condition sought by

Bush's US security doctrine is one where corporate USA enlarges its freedom through investment rights while the world is policed by its armies. The WTO is a key institution in the US foreign policy arsenal. The Doha Round was to be the next step in broadening investment rights in such targeted areas as medicine and intellectual property rights with respect to anti-viral and other modern drugs, the provision of water as a privatized good, and the marketing and production of Western kinds of agricultural products grown with chemicals and patented seeds.[8] The Cancun meeting collapsed when Southern nations refused to accept the US sponsored agenda.

In this new security age, every country is a potential partner (or enemy) for the US. Washington can pick and choose partners, recruiting them by offering large trade, military or development subsidies. It can also discard partners as easily as it builds alliances. It will increasingly try to divide "doubters from loyalists," in Quentin Peel's poignant turn of phrase. Certainly it no longer looks to the Atlantic Alliance to partner and police the world's trouble spots as it once did. As the world's uni-power, it has the military might of its armies and the motivation to wage warfare around the planet without need of many allies or partners. What is in question in many national capitals of the world is the US's moral and political authority. The wider dilemma for Canada is to define the "Canadian path" now that its "close neighbour" status has been downgraded by the Bush security doctrine.

## It Is Not a Question of Liking Us

The first dramatic change to be confronted is that travelling on a Canadian passport no longer guarantees equal treatment for all Canadian citizens. US officials have no hesitation to detain, arrest or expel foreign-born Canadian citizens from the United States, as in the case of the Syrian-born Canadian citizen Mahar Arar being seized while in transit in New York and deported to Syria. US officials will continue to demand that the government of Canada disclose personal information, which appears on Canadian passports. By 2005 the US plans to register every person entering and leaving the country.

It was never the intention of American immigration law to share border management with Canada or Mexico, and US officials have repeatedly asserted that any substantive changes are out of the question.[9] Section 6 of the Charter protects the rights of all Canadians to enter and leave Canada without discrimination. The naturalized Canadian is to be treated no differently from the native-born. Unless it has a strategy of action, it is no longer certain whether the Canadian government, or any other national authority for that matter, will be able to protect its citizens from discriminatory treatment at the hands of US immigration agents. All countries are in a similar quandary because the border rules have been radically altered for all classes of visitors. The most consternation arises from the fact that it is left to the discretion of individual US immigration officers to decide whether an individual's place of birth will provide them entry without fingerprinting and other intrusive aspects of registration. Visitors from around the world are expected to comply with the tough security measures.

Faced with so many micro-changes around border security, Canada requires an effective macro-border strategy to minimize the negative effects of US unilateralism. For much of the recent period, Canadians have relied on the narrow-gauged 1994 Free Trade Agreement as a one-size-fits-all strategy to address its principal border concerns. A commercial agreement works to dumb down the significance of the border by focusing on only one dimension while ignoring all others. Commerce is wrongly characterized as a "seamless web of activity" when it has always been subject to regulation and bureaucratic oversight. The bigger error is the failure to recognize that Canadians and Americans do not inhabit the same security universe. We used to think that as countries entered the post-national era, borders and border management would be relegated to the back burner. No so.

All entrants to the US are now subject to invasive control and tracking procedures. The Immigration and Naturalization Service (INS), which once controlled border entry, no longer exists.[10] It has become part of the Department of Homeland Security, a single department responsible for the interior enforcement of the new rules and procedures, application and surveillance at the border and overseeing immigration services. The tough new rules present line officers with a powerful directive to exercise their discretionary authority and refuse admission to the US where necessary. Heather Segal, chair of the Canadian chapter of the American Immigration Lawyers Association, sees in these changes a shift from a service mentality to an enforcement mindset.[11]

The passport, once primarily a police document to control the movement of people, is again being used as a high-powered security screen. High-tech options are also being looked at because of the incidence of passport identity fraud. Indeed, to counter travel document fraud the Canadian government is looking at computer-encoded, biometric identity cards. A biometric card holder would have their iris photocopied. US authorities are also very interested in this high security device, but the cost of this kind of identity document is prohibitively high.[12] Many Canadian legal authorities believe that mandatory identity cards violates the Charter of Rights and Freedoms. Public opinion is strongly opposed to any government-sponsored identity card.

US Customs and Immigration has announced that it will begin profiling individuals from over twenty countries deemed to be "high risk." Thousands of immigrants who did not register with the INS, now the BCIS, by March 2003 will be expelled or imprisoned. Muslims in particular are being targeted, but many groups from South Asia and Africa will also find their immigration status under review. Arab and Muslim men are required to register with the BCIS. Any individual whose papers are not in order or whom US authorities decide is a security risk will be expelled for "the good of wider security."

Many immigrants from Muslim countries are trying to escape to Canada to begin a new life. In 2001, 3,884 Pakistanis claimed refugee status and more than half were successful.[13] In the first half of 2003, more than a thousand Pakistanis crossed the Canadian border when the US Department of Citizenship and Immigration started its controversial system of turning away anyone who did not have full documentation. With an estimated nine million illegal immigrants in the US, the number of removals and deportations is going to reach record highs.

## Entry-Exit Regulations at the Border
The intent of the US Homeland Security Act is to track, control and monitor the 150 million plus annual visitors to the US, including Canadians and Mexicans. This will require a vast collection of

information. A crucial part of the new initiative is the adoption of "meta-data" standards for electronic information, and a core innovation of this vision of homeland security is the entry-exit data bank. The danger is that these procedures are already being met with a very high non-compliance rate as many visitors have left the US without American customs officials properly recording their departure.

In recent times, when visitors overstayed their visa, these small irregularities were largely overlooked or easily rectified with proper documentation. The new security rules, set out in the Bush government's first "National Strategy for Homeland Security," assume a zero tolerance standard.[14] When fully implemented there will be no exemptions for non-Americans or Americans.

By 2006, homeland security also plans to screen all US citizens buying airline tickets to determine whether the person is a potential security threat. Presently Delta Airlines is experimenting with a pilot project where background security and financial checks will be made on every customer purchasing a ticket. Should the check establish that the individual is a security risk, he or she will be barred from the flight.[15] Many Americans angrily oppose this measure as an invasion of privacy and a violation of their constititutional rights, but it appears that Delta intends to screen all future passengers before they board. Canada has announced that it plans to look seriously at comparable proposals.

The "security is everywhere" mentality applies to Canadian residents with non-Canadian passports. Commonwealth citizens living in Canada have to present documents at the border and US border officials have final discretion in deciding who will enter and who will be turned back. US authorities are weighing the advantages and costs of stationing twenty blimps to monitor, track and record cross-border movement. Israel has deployed similar technology in the Gaza. These high-tech blimps can electronically eavesdrop on all kinds of telecommunications in Mexico and Canada. Once in place they will constitute a vital part of the US meta-data collection of information on any visitor or others at the border and behind it.

US border officials have always had a wide arc of discretionary authority when deciding whether or not to accept NAFTA multi-entry visas for business professionals. Recently many professionals have had to present employment documents upon entering and re-entering the US. Certainly, border rules have become more arbitrary and unpredictable.

Ottawa fully expects to negotiate a special understanding that will partially exempt some Canadians from US security practices. This is a misrepresentation. It is proposing to create a two-tier system that discriminates between Canadian citizens and landed residents. Under this proposal, all landed immigrants will have to register with Canadian authorities when exiting from Canada. US rules will be applied, not by US customs officers, but by their Canadian counterparts.

The decision to discriminate against Canadian residents is unprecedented and most likely illegal. It will unquestionably be subject to a Charter challenge. Ottawa's mistake is to take the pressure off the border and to trade off citizenship rights for no apparently sound reason. The border is not hampering either trade or tourism. By throwing in the towel and agreeing to US security rules, Ottawa has lost any leverage for fundamental change. If there are real slowdowns at the border with US customs officials registering every legal resident of Canada each time they enter the US, then Washington would face mounting domestic pressure from US business leaders to stop this discriminatory practice and ease the waits at border crossings. But again Canada has no clearly articulated strategic set of goals that puts citizenship goals on the same footing as commercial needs.

## Minimal Tolerance for the Best Neighbour

In the past, Canadians living in border communities received a wide margin of tolerance from US officials. In many small border communities, Canadians could enter the US to cross-border shop without formally checking in, as US border agents looked the other way. These kinds of informal arrangements no longer exist post–September 11. Violations, even small infractions, by Canadians or any other visitors to the US will not be condoned. Canadians have yet to process and absorb the new reality. The security-first regulations will have both short- and long-term effects.

The recent arrest of a Quebec man who crossed the border to buy some gas, and his subsequent detainment for more than a month, is a dramatic example of the new practices US authorities are implementing. In this case, the problem arose because the gas station's driveway is in Canada, while the pumps are in the US. Going back and forth had not mattered prior to September 11, but on this day US officials discovered that he had not checked in with US border guards and had foolishly left his rifle in his truck. American customs agents did not treat it as a human error that merited a scolding. Canadians are now regarded by US authorities as alien, visitors without rights and subject to the full force of US law. The Quebec man in question has been barred for life from entering the US. He pleaded guilty to being an illegal alien in the US and chose the lifetime ban rather than a six-month prison sentence.[16] The judge showed no leniency, even though the man lived in a border community. This tough sentence reflects the harsh reality of the US security environment. These substantive changes towards the border and Canada have real impacts and are not simply an inconvenience for border communities.

All of the freshly enacted legal norms shatter the longstanding Canadian illusion that the border somehow does not matter and is insignificant. Nothing could be further from the truth. Canadians will have to adapt to the new regulations and accept that they have been essentially relegated to outsider status inside North America. Canadians have no special rights as far as US authorities are concerned. There is nothing in the US National Strategy for Homeland Security that anticipates any exemption, special treatment or privileges for Canadians. Compliance with US immigration law has to be immediate and full.

## The Immigration Police, Tough New Rules and More Discretion Than Ever

In other areas of US public policy the role and importance of the border as a marker of exclusive national sovereignty has also been broadened, contrary to the theory and practice of economic integration. NAFTA was not meant to dismantle the border for immigration purposes. In 2002 the INS denied immigrant status to over 170,000 immigrants, most at the US southwest border. Under the old rules more than 100,000 immigrants had been removed from the US each year since 1995. Between September 2000 and November 2001 over 300,000 illegal migrants were apprehended on the southwest border. These numbers are expected to increase in the future.

Shortly after NAFTA came into effect, the Clinton administration passed the Illegal Immigration Reform and Immigrant Responsibility Act of 1996 in order to closely monitor and control the cross-border movement of all non-US citizens, or "aliens" as they are termed under US law. The Act required the INS "to collect and record the departure of every alien from the United States and match the records of departure with the record of the alien's arrival in the United States." It was aimed at Canadians and Mexicans who entered the US illegally or remained beyond the permissible time period. The INS estimated that Canada was the fourth largest source of illegal immigrants, with about 120,000 Canadian aliens residing in the US as of 1996. The INS studies also found that about 40 percent of all illegal immigrants enter the US legally but stay without a visa.[17]

This major legislative initiative, the Responsibility Act, represented one of the most comprehensive statutes enacted by Congress within the larger political context of dismantling the US welfare state. It cut the welfare benefits of US citizens and immigrants alike, radically reducing the benefits that non-citizens could claim and redefining their legal rights as well. This watershed legislation removed a wide range of benefits that government had provided to immigrants on more or less the same terms as citizens, including emergency assistance to families, food stamps and Medicaid.[18] These provisions gave state and local governments the authority to determine who was eligible for public benefits. Almost without exception decentralization has lead to cutting immigrants off from benefits they had previously received.

Despite the protest from both Canadian and Mexican governments that this new legislation would impede entries and exits between the three countries, the US Congress remained indifferent to its NAFTA partners. Section 110 of the Act generated a lot of bitter criticism from border communities that wanted US legislators to separate domestic politics from the growing commercial interdependence between the three NAFTA partners and give Canadians and Mexicans a special status under the bill. Their advice carried no weight with US lawmakers. The US congressional view was that it possessed the competence to control and regulate the movement of people across US borders and nothing in the NAFTA limited its right to do so. A tiny concession achieved by the Canadian government was to defer implementation of the Act until March 30, 2001. Now, with the passage of the Homeland Security Act, the new rules and regulations apply to Canadians as well as everyone else. Canada's NAFTA status did not merit any special consideration.

If Canada is to develop a strategic border culture, it needs to reposition itself in North America and defend its side of the Great Border. To this end there are three basic principles that should be committed to memory and then acted on.

## Asymmetry, Power and Fate: Globalization and the End of Borders Narrative

The first principle is that for smaller countries, *sharing a border with a more powerful country should not be confused with voicelessness or powerlessness*. Countries such as Canada, where the asymmetries with the US are unbridgeable, belong to an elite group of nations with multiple borders and frontiers. Asymmetry of power is always troubling in foreign policy matters, as Russia-Ukraine, Mexico–United States, India-Pakistan and Brazil-Argentina relations aptly demonstrate.

We need to rethink the future of borders in an innovative way in order to understand these dynamics and why globalization has not punched holes in every border in the world. The border retains much of its functionality in the EU and for many other countries that use their borders to generate revenues. These countries want to hold on to this venerable institution and the continual cash flow that it generates. In 2000, Canada collected $22 billion in GST and PST at the border. Any country with a sales tax relies on the border as a collection agency. A conservative estimate would put border revenues worldwide in excess of the one billion mark. However, some countries are less sure of the border's economic functionality.

Some border crossings resemble armed camps, while others minimize police presence. Do not be fooled though. The border police are always close by and ready to enforce state authority, be it fairly or arbitrarily. Around the globe, borders continue to be places of tension, passageways to freedom and escape routes from repressive regimes. Border guards may be armed with whips, truncheons or worse to keep refugees out or move them in. Along the Afghanistan-Pakistan frontier, hordes of refugees have desperately tried to force their way past the border police. Thousands of people routinely die at sea or along land borders in an effort to escape poverty or despotism.

It is widely reported that Taliban operatives are hiding among sympathizers in the mountainous region that straddles the 1,500-mile border between Afghanistan and Pakistan. Border regions are often difficult to govern and have been safe havens for rebels, terrorists and bandits, but also ordinary people seeking a better life. Since 1995, experts estimate that over one thousand Mexicans and other Latin Americans have been shot trying to cross into the US from Mexico.[19] Untold numbers of political refugees have been killed attempting to cross land and sea frontiers.

Few need to be reminded that in the twentieth century millions have gone to war to defend the integrity of their borders from armed invasion, ethnic cleansing, guerrilla attacks, blitzkreigs and civil wars. The numbers who have perished is staggering. In the wars of the twentieth century alone, more than 62 million civilians have been killed and more than 20 million military personnel died. In the 1990s, two million perished in Afghanistan, 1.5 million were slaughtered in the Sudan, 800,000 were murdered in Rwanda, a half a million in Angola, and 200,000 in Guatemala, to name some of the worst killing grounds in recent times.[20] Millions more lost their lives in border conflicts between Ethiopia and Eritrea, in the Israeli-Palestinian conflict, Chechnya, Sri Lanka, southern Turkey, Kosovo and Northern Ireland. Modern industrial warfare has become a global industry for professional armies and nation-states on every continent. The chances of dying in a border conflict have not diminished in the least as borders remain primary killing grounds throughout the globe.

As long as there are nation-states, borders will not disappear from history. Canadians have principally thought of their border with the US in its commercial dimension, but now Canada requires an integrated strategy that is not commercially centred. Developing a new understanding of the institutions, processes and policy outcomes that ensure policy stability will depend on our capacity to form a consensus around the strategy of being onside or offside, issue by issue, and to act on principle rather than simple expediency.

## Spillovers and Relative Sovereignty

The second principle is that *the doctrine of formal sovereignty has never effectively protected a weaker nation from the designs of those stronger*. The complex creed of absolute sovereignty has long preoccupied many of the best Anglo-American minds and European experts in the modern period because great powers have never abandoned claims to domestic autonomy, let alone their right to pursue their interests globally. In theory the sovereign state was a hardy creature protected by the interstate system of international relations. Countries were to butt out and not intervene in the internal affairs of another. The external dimensions of sovereignty were very difficult to protect through the principle of non-intervention. Krasner is right to add that sovereignty has never meant the existence of a single hierarchy of authority domestically or internationally.[21] There was always the idea that in a plural world countries and civilizations needed to co-exist and develop institutions of cooperation and multilateralism. Growing interdependence throughout the twentieth century forced governments to protect national interests and strengthen democratic institutions by privileging the nation-state as the formal seat of national political power. Sovereignty has always been negotiated as an exercise in applied statecraft.

John Keane reminds us that the territorial-based nation-state, interlocked with others, has not only pursued its self-interest as much as possible but has also been socialized by the behaviour of other states. Custom, protocol and legal norms emerged and all countries became linked by a global framework governing diverse subjects such as war crimes, the right of non-interference and rules about trade and commerce. These state-enforced limits on sovereignty have come to be called "international civil society."[22] The growth of international law evidences the need to codify and institutionalize applied sovereignty globally and regionally.[23]

Even prior to the invocation of free trade's deep economic integration logic, national autonomy was diminished by cross-border spillovers and challenges to sovereignty from militarism, nationalism and imperialism, and the movements of refugees and immigrants. All countries have exhibited a cynical and ethics-free mentality about exploiting global immigration flows for their own immediate advantages. Industrialized countries routinely tighten border controls to control global immigration flows in the name of self-interest or national security.[24] They want to pick and choose who gets in and who is kept out. Skilled immigrants with a university degree are more likely to get the green light from an immigration officer than a poorly educated, barely literate agricultural worker. Still, many countries have welcomed asylum seekers, guest workers, visitors, students and business professionals when it was in their interests to do so.

A high-profile country for immigration, Canada admits close to 300,000 immigrants annually, and it could admit more if there was the political will to do so. So, from a citizenship perspective, the border is a high priority and as important as the commercial gate to the future of Canada as a society of diverse peoples. Control and management of the border for citizenship purposes has become more important as global immigration flows have increased markedly through the 1990s and into the new century.

The difference between the millions of immigrants who come to Canada by choice and the desperate plight of political refugees who arrive fleeing human rights abuses in their own countries is dramatic from a human rights perspective. The demand to admit more refugees is constant. Canada processes between 20,000 and 30,000 refugee applications annually and provides social support and an administrative body to process these claims.

In 2001 Canada received a record number of applications from asylum seekers, 44,500, a 20 percent increase over the number of claims in 2000. Ninety percent of refugees arrive with false documents, having had to escape their homeland without official papers. The Canadian immigration authorities recognized the claims of 13,336 as bone fide refugees and another 5,430 cases were abandoned, withdrawn or otherwise closed. Officially, Ottawa claims a success rate of 47 percent for all applications referred to the Immigration and Refugee Board (IRB). In fact, the approval rate is about 30 percent excluding administratively closed and withdrawn cases. Canada had about 14,000 asylum seekers from Pakistan, Sri Lanka, Zimbabwe, Congo-Kinshasa,

Colombia and China in 2001. Over 76 percent of these political refugees were given legal status in Canada.

Since the end of 2001, Canada has altered asylum procedures and given Citizenship and Immigration officers the power to rule a claimant ineligible for refugee status "if the claimant had a criminal record, posed a threat to national security, or had been recognized as a refugee in another country," such as the US. Ottawa now has given the Department of Citizenship and Immigration the power to remove that individual without the right to file a refugee claim to a higher tribunal should that person be refused refugee status in the US.[25] Under pressure from the Bush administration, Canada has taken a step backward and made it more difficult for political refugees to settle here.

The ethical questions surrounding acceptance of refugees from wartorn regions have forced states to look beyond their borders. It is not only commerce that dilutes the ideal of sovereignty, but also human rights issues. Bar-raising international legal norms are predicated on the global community becoming involved in the internal business of other countries to protect human rights. Humanitarian aid provides a powerful rationale to assist people stricken by natural disasters, from floods to crop failure. Nation-state sovereignty has been curbed, modified and shared as countries become more interconnected and social movements demand an end to beggar-thy-neighbour borders.

The growth of international human rights law is the most visible and powerful restraint on national sovereignty in the modern period. Law, even more than commerce, reaches behind the security-tight frontiers of the nation-state, trying to hold countries accountable for what occurs behind and beyond their national frontiers.[26] The theory of relative sovereignty and international standards of enforcement frequently bear little relationship to each other. International covenants have the force of moral suasion, but lack the political clout to hold to account those responsible for crimes against humanity, genocide and terrorism. No country is absolutely sovereign and the negotiation of sovereignty remains essentially a political act rather than an objective legal standard that is enforceable everywhere.[27]

The International Criminal Court recently created by the

General Assembly of the UN to apprehend and prosecute individuals charged with crimes against humanity, genocide and egregious violations of human rights is a singular new development. It is a response to the horrifying number of civilians massacred on many continents. An international criminal court is one of the crucial missing links in the international legal system. The International Court of Justice at the Hague only handles cases between states and not between individuals. Now individuals can be prosecuted and brought to justice for war crimes for which no one in the past was held accountable.

The establishment and authority of the International Criminal Court was opposed by the Clinton and Bush governments, who refused to recognize its jurisdiction to try US citizens charged with past or future war crimes.[28] In the present era, constraining US power and requiring it to adhere to international rules has become a top priority for the international community. As the fallout from the Iraq war affects the global political landscape, Canada has yet to make up its mind as to whether, in Robert Kagan's terms, it values hard power and military strength more than soft-power tools such as human security and multilateralism.[29] A fork in the road has been reached, and Canadians have to make up their minds collectively on this most basic question.

## Protecting the US Nation: Neighbourliness a Scarce Commodity

The third principle is that *even with its fundamentals down pat, no border can be expected to protect a country's sovereignty; only democracy and political will have real effect*. During the modern period the majority of Canadians have become instinctively "soft" nationalists as a defensive reflex against growing US influence on Canadian life. Soft nationalists have been committed to the UN system and a multilateral world order that had rules, predictability and limits on superpowers. Ordinary Canadians want to maintain access to the US market and are equally committed to stronger sovereign practices. The two free trade agreements punched holes in the border and rendered it less of a regulatory gate.

Other European countries experiencing similarly high levels of economic integration also discovered that economic forces that are supposed to make public authority and private markets automatically converge rarely do so. Canada's political culture changes very slowly in comparison to the dynamics of powerful market forces. Cumulatively, these persistent differences have had an enormous impact on defining who Canadians are. The Canadian psyche has yet to absorb the compelling idea that convergence and divergence can occur simultaneously and it is the "net effects" that matter in the end. We have yet to make this the cornerstone of Canada-US relations.

The most powerful forces reshaping Canada's political agenda are domestic, not global, and as its new accent on social pluralism intensifies cleavages from race, language and class, Canada and the US have grown more dissimilar than similar. Diversity and multiculturalism work together in Canada to provide a large constituency with an appetite for social programs. In the United States, the twin axes of modern diversity and a legal culture of individual rights work against race and class, and "interact in ways that undermine support for the welfare state."[30] North Americans should pause to reflect why this is so.

## Public Authority Against Private Markets

Even though 80 percent of Canadians live within 160 kilometres of the US border, deep differences between the two countries persist. Take the case of Toronto and Buffalo—close neighbours, but worlds apart in terms of health care, taxes, job security, garbage collection, road maintenance, culture and job creation. However, when these communities are in dire need and require funds to build their infrastructure or pay for social services, they both wave the flag of their regional identity to gain national attention and political leverage. US states look to Washington to solve their fiscal crises, while provinces expect Ottawa to provide more funds. It is ridiculous to think it might be otherwise.

Some differences seem unimportant. But the fact that Canadians support twelve newspapers in Toronto compared to just two or three in any large American city remains substantial. Access to information and analysis is very different on both sides of the border. Some of the differences are significant and sharply set us apart. When Canadians were asked, "If you could vote in the 2000 United States election, would you vote for Bush or Gore?" 60 percent chose Gore and only 14 percent were for Bush.[31] Immediately after 9/11, Canadians were ready to compromise their sovereignty to improve border security. Polls showed that 80 percent of Canadians would back such measures. When Canadians were asked in October 2002 whether Canada should bring its policies to conform more closely with those in the US on health care, 87 percent responded no; on the environment, 75 percent were negative; on financial harmonization of Canada's banking practices, 64 percent were opposed; on immigration and refugee policy, 63 percent were against. In the area of taxation, where Canadians might have been expected to vote for a lesser tax load, 58 percent were against harmonization with the US.[32]

With very little regional variation, 67 percent of Canadians said that they did not have the same values as Americans. The West, Ontario and Quebec asserted the primacy of the border over markets. Western Canadians' views were little different from those of central Canadians. When it was asked, "In the future, will we become more like the US?" only 35 percent agreed, a drop from 49 percent in October 1998. The same poll found that Quebec's response was little different from English Canada's. The claim that politics is waning and markets rule is wrong. Small qualitative differences between the two neighbours have grown larger, not diminished in importance.

## The Authentic Border

Canada's powerfully embedded political culture remains the authoritative and constant "forty-ninth parallel" that separates these societies. Institutions, values and all kinds of practices are inescapably public and more resistant to supply and demand signals than any contemporary theory of economics can explain. Thus, the demands of territory on identity and self-knowledge are surprisingly undiminished by cross-border effects and globalization. US influence on what Canadians think and believe could decline further as we become more visibly un-American in terms of equality, diversity and the social bond. For Canada, focusing on issues of general concern, such as the security of others, and not simply on narrow economic interests is the beginning of a process of re-orientation. Meanwhile, the political culture of the US will take that country in another direction entirely.

For Washington, border politics with Canada are low-cost, largely non-strategic and a diplomatic no-brainer. No American politician ever needs to compare US economic performance to that of Canada. US political careers do not depend on the successful negotiation of the Canadian–American relationship. No US president is going to face the wrath of Congress because Ottawa is angry or slighted by US policy. No US official passes a sleepless night worrying about Canada. The Canada–United States relationship appears to be one of the easiest to manage in the world, because it has been institutionalized through so many cross-border networks, associational ties, intergovernmental relations, and formal and informal practices.

But the political divide that separates the two countries remains enormous even when these continental neighbours follow remarkably parallel policies. In Lawrence Martin's choice epithet, penned two decades ago, the "tie of spirit" has never acquired any formidable policy legs in Washington, even in the area of commercial policy where the two countries have the most at stake.

As trade disputes have grown in importance, Canada's policy elites have yet to realize that there are no legal grounds on which to hide from the US regulatory trade police—not for Canada, not for Europe, not for any country. NAFTA does not provide a protective legal shield, nor do dispute panel decisions provide finality, as the US has the right to bring forward new cases when it loses. Without a clear definition of what a subsidy is, the NAFTA legal regime remains tilted in favour of protecting US interests. It does not matter a wit that the Americans offer the largest subsidies in the world to their farmers, $54 billion (US) in 1999 compared to $3.9 billion for Canada. Nor does it matter in Washington that close to 25 percent of US agricultural production is subsidy-supported, whereas in Canada the figure is 20 percent.[33]

Trade politics have long been a bipartisan staple in the US. Americans believe they have the legal right to gather "evidence" against any Canadian competitor. Washington will decide what the "security danger" is and how it should be "neutralized" for commercial ends. With commerce so politicized, the Great Border that joins and separates the Republic and the Confederation can be quickly transformed into a flashpoint of tension, conflict and disagreement.

At the heart of the softwood lumber dispute, the US Commerce Department wants to reserve the right to determine whether or not Canada's forest-rich provinces have fully complied with its standards. US forestry interests backed by the Department of Commerce are asking Canada to surrender sovereignty over this key policy domain. The Canadian Wheat Board, which is responsible for the international marketing of Canadian grains and a competitor to US corporate giants like Cargill, is singled out for "unfairly" subsidizing Canada's grain exports because it protects Canadian farmers and stabilizes export prices. The very raison d'être of the Canadian Wheat Board challenges US global market thinking.

In the world of US trade politics, America's borders are constructed by law and geography but are politicized by self-interest. Now more than ever the Homeland Security Act has re-nationalized the US side of the border and explicitly extended it into Canadian domestic space as part of its stated need to "protect our nation's critical infrastructure."[34]

Canada's elites have rarely been self-consciously innovative about the border and US policy in general. They have never gone as far as President Richard Nixon, who spoke with characteristic bluntness about Washington's closest neighbour, "It is time for us to recognize that we have very separate identities, that we have significant differences, and nobody's interests are furthered when these realities are obscured."[35] Too often, in an effort to escape the dumbing-down effect of unequal power relations, Canada's policymakers have turned into deadbeat conformists rather than determined innovators. They have not recognized that, in the end, political will is the only effective guide through the high-pitched noise of trade and security disputes.

# 6. Active Localisms: Seeing Beyond One's Home and Native Land

> "Nothing makes the earth seem so spacious as to have friends at a distance; they make the latitudes and longitudes." —Henry David Thoreau, from a letter to Mrs. Castleton (1843)

## Identity, Place, Citizenship and Modernity

In this obsessively commercial age, we are left with the question that launched this enquiry: Do borders any longer matter, economically, culturally or politically in a security age? The great North American border was constructed on real and imaginary symbols of nationhood. In the US the national narrative of the border was front and centre in the process of nation-building. For Americans, sovereignty and citizenship have been inseparable since the founding revolution, an inalienable right guaranteed by their constitution. For Canadians, citizenship and sovereignty have also been equally indivisible as a public good, a foundation stone of Canada's constitutional culture of "peace, order and good government." For Canadians the border has never been a lightning rod of territorial ambition. Instead, many of the most important aspects of Canada's sovereignty had to be negotiated internationally.

Globalization has made the border more, not less, important for security and immigration, for all countries. For citizenship purposes the border is the symbolic and real manifestation of sovereignty. Your passport is your legal identity without which you are not free to travel as a citizen. For political refugees, acquisition of citizenship is a primary means of reintegration and beginning a new life. Commerce cannot forge a country and it never has. Trade is only one part of the larger picture of integration.

The molar-grinding morbidity of Canada as an improbable nation continues to haunt its opinion leaders from all classes. The implication is that if the present high levels of integration continue, Canada will not exist in another twenty-five years. But no other country joined at the hip to a neighbour by geography and relentless commercialism has seen its public authority as an autonomous entity expire. It has certainly not happened in Europe nor has it happened here. Still, from George Grant's celebrated *Lament for a Nation*, to Tom Courchene's *From Heartland to the North American Region State*, many of English Canada's best minds believe that Canada's disappearance is immanent.[1] How misguided.

Quebecers, with no country but much desirous of one, do not share this pessimism. They are not chronic doubters unsure of their nationality and identity. Quebecers have devoted almost a half century to asserting their individuality and unique collective citizenship rights. The contrast with the Toronto-based print and electronic media, which is most often consumed by self-doubt, is stark. Its morbidity is a crippling disease of the body politic, a "psychic dichotomy" in McLuhan's powerful imagery, of elites who have never developed a strategic view of America.

When Canada's knowledge-based elites see the world in narrow ideological terms, corporate decisions are made without regard for Canadian laws and conventions of business behaviour or the sensibilities of local communities or governments. Without any sense of strategic positioning, they fall head first into the American orbit and look for favour from Washington. They have no idea of how to be good friends and allies at a distance. Such policy communities facilitate the restructuring of the state and the transnational legal order that looms so large on the radar screen of law firms, banks, accounting and consultancy firms, and financial organizations.[2]

The elite want to call it a day for Canada and are unwilling to grasp the basic challenge. The rise of the modern nation-state required a wholesale change in the mental equipment that people drew upon to imagine this different political community.[3] To flourish in a globalized world, nation-states must learn to adapt to a different fundamental entirely—a planet where the spatial dimension of sovereignty and state power are more important than ever, but under radically different conditions. Canada's economic elites only know how to envision the border as a one-dimensional gate and not as a multi-purpose institution for identity and citizenship purposes.[4] They cannot get beyond the commerce-first border and see how important it is to anchor citizenship as a principal leg of Canadian foreign policy. As the Great Border is becoming tighter and the policies of homeland security more inflexible, there are strong dynamics pushing the Canadian government to maximize its foreign policy resources for democratic ends.

A decade of experience with powerful integration pressures in North America and elsewhere has demonstrated that it is the lived space behind the border that is essential for local networks of self-knowledge, social solidarity and maintaining a competitive edge. Countries that have restructured their industries success-fully and adapted to the new conditions, regionally and globally, have enlisted the border as a strategic device. Countries that have ignored their domestic markets have seen their industries spiral into decline. In this regard, the restructuring of the US rust and sunbelts, and other regional economies is significant. These adaptations have often reversed the hollowing out of corporate USA. Is this not another powerful example of border effects? Why has Canada been so slow to learn this kind of critical public policy lesson from its neighbour?

## Social Space and Border Effects: The Most Critical Dimension of All

Canadian political parties find themselves boxed in, fighting not at the border but behind it for resources, markets, access, security and sovereignty. It cannot be taken for granted that Canadian state officials have the confidence, expertise and agility to adapt to the new agenda. Saying no to Bush's requests to send Canadian forces to Iraq may have liberated Canadians from their old mental habits. It was a not a huge risk when Canadian public opinion was firmly in the "no" camp and Canada would not find itself isolated and exposed. It was easier to make the tough decision because Ottawa was part of a dissenting group of allies lead by France, Germany and Mexico, among others. So politically it was a logical step, and psychologically it was a turning point for Canada.

Some informed Canadians have understood that Canadian opposition to this US policy is a legitimate expression of the will of a democratic ally, and dissent should not be curbed. Because of the need to stimulate the global economy, reconciling political differences and toning down rhetoric is one of the new initiatives of the Bush administration. With the American occupation of Iraq in deep trouble, the G-8 is going to try to bury their differences. In the tough words of Fred Bergsten, head of the Washington-based Institute for International Affairs, "looking cross-eyed at each other" is diplomatically stupid.

Bush has made some mild overtures to repair fences with France, its most relentless critic. However, the process of burying the hatchet will be long and difficult. As the material and human costs mount in Iraq and support for the war declines at home, the US is facing pressure from the right and the left. The military wants the tools to get the job done quickly; the left critics of the Bush administration are calling for an end of the occupation of Iraq and no more "regime changes."

Six months after the announced cessation of the Iraq war, US displeasure with Canada was at best a minor rift. Prime Minister Chretien's scripted musings to reporters at the end of May 2003 was hardly evidence of diplomatic backtracking as some of his critics had charged. His off-the-cuff remarks that assailed the US deficit and his supposedly candid statements about differences with the US president were just smart politics. In a security-driven age, strategic positioning without fixed commitments is the optimal course for a middle power such as Canada. There is a constituency outside of the business community that is comfortable with being offside. Canadians are not ready to accept a role as deputy sheriff in the coalition of the obedient.

Refusing to support the war in Iraq was an important step for modern Canada, but it is uncertain whether it will begin a long-term reorientation of Canadian-US relations. Already the political elites are showing signs of returning to their "father knows best" mentality, with plans to support the North American missile defence system. Paul Martin, while Canada's prime-minister-in-waiting, publicly expressed interest in it, and he could easily sign on as a loyalist. With national unity and Quebec off the agenda and having a surplus to spend, Canada-US relations have shot to the top of Martin's policy agenda.

Initially it appeared that he was still operating in ad hoc mode, banging off the Bush administration's last initiative, be it the establishment of a North American Command (Northcom), expedited arrangements for trucks and visitors at the border, changes to Canada's immigration laws for naturalized and native-born Canadians, or increased security checks on Canadian citizens. Canada's new security Act was passed into law in record time, authorizing Canada to use security warrants against individuals deemed "security threats." In 2003, Ottawa was holding five Muslim immigrants in prison without charges: one since June 2000, two since mid July 2001 and two others since 2002. The defendants are not allowed to see the evidence and do not have the right of cross-examination. The proceedings occur before a judge in secret. Only the prosecution speaks and the judge has to decide the case, without the accused having the right of due process.[5]

Canada has no coherent policy with respect to US homeland security and in some instances federal departments are actively undercutting each other. For instance, Immigration Canada recently arrested a group of Pakistani students on grounds of national security, but the RCMP leaked to the press that there were no grounds to detain and charge them.[6]

There has been no public audit of the impact of US homeland security measures and their multiple impacts on Canadian sovereignty. In the area of defence, Canada's military wants to be part of the US revolution in rapid, highly mobile strategic defence response. It wants firepower and personnel to "plug into" the latest in US military thinking. It wants a lot of money so that it too can move around the world in step with the latest operational and technological concepts of American warfare. It is going to pressure Ottawa for more funds and a larger defence role. Certainly Washington has a coherent big vision of its security while Ottawa scrambles to keep ahead of the curve. Martin needs to do much more than operate in piecemeal fashion like his old boss. Canada can't optimize its assets or play a more effective role internationally if it lacks forethought, planning and skilled positioning.

Being upfront with "Sam" will require a time of testing and self-education, both for the public and Canada's political class. Canadians are not good at problem-solving when it comes to conflict with the US, nor at defending their national strategic interests. Canada's political class would prefer to operate by stealth and make agreements for the new economic and security agenda with US officials outside the glare of public scrutiny. But if the new Martin government understands the need to have the US as a friend at a distance and uses strategic positioning to anchor Canadian policy in a human security and international citizenship agenda, it will quickly see the advantages of being an outsider.

Canada needs to play its cards close to its chest and does not want to be taken for granted by Washington. It has to find ways to optimize its leverage, speak with moral and political authority and act on its vital security interests. In an age of empire where the rule of might erodes long-established norms of international law, the priority for middle power countries has to be to rebuild the international system of cooperation, reinforce multilateralism and strengthen the institutions of collective responsibility. Canada by itself is a secondary power, but as part of a larger alliance of nation-states it can have significant effect and influence internationally.

## Political Refugees and the 9/11 Security Border

If Canadians accept the erroneous proposition that the North American people share a common future destined by geography, the tighter border could push Canada to seek favours from Washington once again. The Canada-US Refugee Agreement signed in early December 2002, which commits Canada to turn political refugees back to US authorities with their much stricter rules, is of this sort. Human security, which Canada prizes as a fundamental premise, has been significantly compromised with this agreement. Canada's Immigration and Refugee Protection Act, which passed into law in record time on November 1, 2001, provides the government with very broad powers to decide who is inadmissible, expands the detention power of special warrants and, most importantly, reduces access to judicial reviews of the minister's security decisions.[7] As a result, the number of political refugees detained by authorities has increased dramatically in the last year. Since the new legislation came into effect, five persons have already been held in preventive detention without formal charges being laid for a total of forty-five months.[8]

The number of removals from Canada was likely to be higher in 2003 than at any time in the previous decade.[9] Fears about the border closing down and trade between the two countries coming to a standstill are largely a smokescreen. The decisive battle is over Canadian foreign policy and how it will continue to reflect Canadian diversity and multiculturalism. Certainly Canadian foreign policy has not made the linkage explicit enough, and the border and immigration will loom larger in the future than it has to date.

Under the UN Refugee Convention, Canada is obligated to accept and screen political refugees and ensure that their claims are properly processed. US homeland security drives a wedge between Canada's international obligations and Washington's desire to act alone outside of this international convention if necessary. US authorities have given every indication that its new rules of homeland defence override the UN Convention on asylum seekers and political refugees.

Australia has already ended court scrutiny of migration decisions. In 2001 the John Howard government refused to allow passengers on the *Tampa* to come ashore and be processed as political refugees, defying the UN Convention on Refugees to which it is a signatory. It ran roughshod over its international obligations and no Australian court was able to order their release.[10] Howard even denied the International Red Cross access to board the vessel to provide the most elementary humanitarian aid.

The force of the Patriot Act is even more aggressive, undermining the constitutional rights of due process, right to trial, and no cruel and unusual punishment, or self-incrimination. It gives American authorities similar powers to detain immigrants, but goes beyond the Australian template. Under US law, authorities are able to detain immigrants without legal counsel or legal rights. Hundreds of immigrants from Arab countries have been detained, many for up to eight months before being cleared of terrorist connections. Their families were not told of their whereabouts and the US government even denied that they were being detained.

According to an internal study by the Office of the Inspector General, a part of the US Justice Department, "not one was charged with any political activity."[11] The US security state is in full ascendancy and citizen harassment no longer in its infancy. Violation of the Fourth Amendment's protection against "unreasonable searches and seizures" is made easier and commonplace. Furthermore, since 9/11, Congress has chosen not to defend the rights of Americans against all the kinds of electronic surveillance that security agencies regularly conduct without a court order.[12]

## Canada's Best Face?

In the security domain, Canada has *de facto* accepted much of the American standard as its own. Though not exactly to the same level, it comes uncomfortably close in giving Canadian immigration authorities increased executive power at the expense of the courts and other branches of government. The new management strategy is based on the bad idea that goods should move but a large class of people are to be kept out. There will be little room for compassionate policing. When Ottawa can't or won't choose an independent course of action, the US will impose its policies on its too accommodating neighbour. This is the reason why Canada needs to articulate a clear self-interest. Under the former minister of foreign affairs, Lloyd Axworthy, Canada invested a lot of time and energy on international solidarity in the context of human security based on humanitarian principles. In the aftermath of Bush's triumphalism, there is much less of a commitment to put Canada's best face forward.

Ultimately these highly visible kinds of border effects are about power and the geopolitical structure of the continent. Although Canadian border guards aren't likely to shoot people, the US war on terror has become a war on immigrants, not as a hypothetical proposition but as an immediate reality. Canada is less likely to act in full compliance with its international obligations if it adopts US security rules that impose few restraints on police and immigration authorities. The Bush doctrine aims to keep the courts at arm's length and to intimidate asylum seekers.

Things can only deteriorate further in an era of global homeland security.

There will be more political refugees and immigrants wanting to come to Canada. The border by itself cannot protect Canada's sovereignty and ensure that asylum seekers arrive safely and are processed fairly under Canadian and international human rights law. Canadians have to make this a priority.

Applied sovereignty is the big idea of the global era. Absolute sovereignty has rarely existed except for imperial nations, but applied sovereignty is within the reach of all countries large and small. We have to act on it through our institutions and values to protect our self-interest. The border is like a political membrane through which people, goods and even ideas must traverse in real and virtual time. Borders have to be understood as social constructs, and it is the space behind the border that matters the most—the self-knowledge of institutions, the know-how created by social capital and, most critically, the recognition and support for social diversity. These are the dynamics that determine who we are.

Canadians are suspicious of market forces that minimize equality and attack identity concerns. Citizenship resides in the social bond not in a globalization that distorts the priorities of public authority. Taking defensive measures against harsh and relentless border effects is in the interest of citizens and non-citizens alike. As an immigrant nation supporting the institution of citizenship with full social rights, Canada has not followed the US lead of restricting access to public benefits, entitlements and protection for legal permanent residents.

The US now has some of the most restrictive legislation against non-citizens of any industrial country, while Canada is one of the most immigrant friendly.[13] Immigrants and refugees in Canada are protected by the Charter of Rights and Freedoms, and eligible for health care and social security. They are eligible for a rent subsidy, social housing, child tax benefits, grants and loans for higher education, and job training. Asylum seekers have not all but many benefits.

In contrast, the US has rationed its benefits for citizenship. Since the 1966 dismantling of US welfare benefits, permanent resident aliens have been "denied federal health insurance, nutrition benefits, welfare and related work benefits and aid to the aged and disabled."[14] From these cuts alone it is estimated that the reform law generated over $20 billion in savings. Spillover effects hit hardest kids born in the US with one or more foreign parents. There has also been a big reduction of health, education and social assistance benefits for them. On the most critical issue of citizenship rights and entitlements, there is no room for ambiguity. Deepening the North American partnership remains a far-off reality with little strategic, economic or intellectual substance.

# EPILOGUE: THE BLIND SPOT
# OF CULTURAL DISTINCTIVENESS

## The Diversity beneath Our Skins

In his compelling study of the approach of the first millennium, George Duby, in *Les Traces de Nos Peurs, An 1000 An 2000,* saw a parallel between the Middle Ages and the beginning of the third millennium. Duby elegantly reminds us that medieval poverty did not mean isolation and exclusion. The impoverished were supported by strong mutual obligations and solidarity-building institutions. Medieval men and women existed in an extreme state of peril, facing conditions of impoverishment comparable to the poorest people subsisting today in the sub-Saharan region of Africa. What gave them hope, in Duby's words, were "*les mécanismes de solidarité communs*" [the mechanisms of common solidarity]. The great fear of a thousand years ago was not the imposition of markets but the loss of solidarity—the common bonds and commitments among groups and individuals.

This historical parallel is, at best, only partially accurate. Modern North Americans have always been disposed to reach outwards towards the hemisphere. A lively and acute interest in other cultures has always been one of the defining elements in the imagination of North America's writers, artists and musicians. The unexpected success of the "Buena Vista Social Club," a fabulous group of Havana-based musicians playing the music of an older generation of Cubans, is powerful evidence that in an era without putative borders, cultural flows can only increase in significance.

Our rich diversity lies beneath our skins. We are not indifferent to each other, but without a shared history, language and experiences, active localisms continue to define our daily routines. So far the creative fusion that would help us care more about the hemisphere or the continent and its incipient multiculturalisms has made only selective inroads on who we are and our citizenship identities. When they return home in the evening, North Americans live in worlds apart. Despite all the growth in trade and capital flows, and the diffusion of mass culture, we remain a continent of solitudes, curious about each other but little more.

In the American imagination, Canada's place remains a troubled one, too often a seemingly permanent blind spot, both dull and uninteresting. Discerning Canadians have a powerful mental image of the Midwest, New York and California. We are not geographical illiterates. We understand in a basic way the great diversity of US regionalism and the strong American attachment to local identity. Canadian novelists such as Carol Shields, Jacques Godbout, Barbara Gowdy, David Adams Richards and Guy Vanderhaege would not confuse New England with Arkansas. But our human geography does not register in the American imagination.

In Sena Jeter Naslund's powerfully evocative novel, *Ahab's Wife*, we are unintentionally provided a glimpse of Canada's troubled non-existence in the American narrative. We are designated as "the Dismals" and likened to Alabama, as something natural and immediate. "A beautiful aberration in the lay of the land.... A section mysteriously lowered, strewn with boulders, ferny, mossy, cooler—the vegetation, they say, typical of Canada.... An eternal place, disjunct with climate, the time, and its location."[1] Here is but a minor example of a much larger set of issues. We remain a continent of cultural and social diversity with so many longitudes and latitudes of separation at the border and behind it.

It was in the early 1980s that Theodore Levitt published his seminal paper on globalization and markets.[2] He argued that new media and technology would alter consumerism and that people's tastes would converge. Global marketing took the business world by storm and promised that nothing could stand in the way of its mass marketing powers and saturation advertising campaigns designed to squash local resistance. Today the big global brands aren't growing as they used to and local producers are giving Coke and Pepsi a run for their market share.

The issue that we need to think about a great deal is how and why the global information age has transformed once docile consumers of news and information into an agitated, highly opinionated citizenry. There is an appetite for a culture of dissent based on more public participation, more education, more debate and, above all else, more public accountability of international organizations. In a world dominated by new information technologies and complex global financial flows, dynamic and complex global cultural movements of people, media, texts and ideas exhibit an impressive array of agenda-setting powers.

We are still in the early stages of the global dissent movement, and the peak of the cycle is far off. Mass mobilization and the influence of the global public is stronger than it was a decade ago because the interstate system has transformed the multiple and diverse sources of people power. Traditional exercise of authority is being contested up and down the line, and in this bifurcated global system, transnational organization has lost the authority and legitimacy it once enjoyed. The popular perception is that nation-states do not have the political will to conduct public life competently. We are in an age of the "smart citizen," where the location and exercise of authority is being changed by the way policies and activism are understood. The global public feels itself empowered to "interfere" in the way policies are framed and implemented.

States no longer control their international agendas and greater uncertainty is the result. When the structure of authority relations is so contested, civic compliance based on loyalty to a single nation-state cannot be taken for granted. The present dynamism for further transformation has hardly run its course, and the old hierarchies have been largely overtaken by the anti-globalization movement and global cultural flows of ideas, peoples and information.

Significantly, the idea of a pluralistic continental culture in which Canadians, Americans and Mexicans are an integral part is nowhere in sight. Mass consumerism will always be a thin adhesive to build any kind of viable North American community, because too many Mexicans, Canadians and Americans are excluded from its materialistic orbit. So, in the end, we are left with the contrived iconography of North America, the old standbys such as ketchup, maple syrup and salsa—barometers of just how disparate our lived experiences really are.[3] Our common cultural universal is the ubiquitous "burger," and even that has many local contenders.

## Active Localisms, a Rooted Globalism and the Continent's Political Bureaucracies

Some years ago, S.D. Clark, the one-time doyen of Canadian sociology, captured the essential relationship between geography and state structure that had pushed Canada and the United States to adopt such profoundly different models of state-market relations. Although he never explained why the continent's political bureaucracies chose to exploit human and physical geography so differently, it is significant that they did, and elites to this day use their geography in strikingly dissimilar ways. This decision has resulted in many consequences for the development of each society. In part, Clark reduced the differences to the following:

> Geography, which favoured individual enterprise and limited political interference in the conduct of economic, social and religious affairs over a large part of the continent [the United States], favoured on this part of the continent [Canada] large scale bureaucratic forms of organization and widespread intervention by the state.[4]

Clark's insight is valuable because it reveals as pure conjecture the implication that the irreversible pull of geography, the universal laws of free trade or even best-practice information technology could be an alternative base for a North America of regions. So far, integration pressures have not supported any such holistic environment, nor given birth to a set of loyalties that transcends national, class and ethnic divisions. Groups and interests capable of making North America more than a fuzzy idea are not on the radar screen and Canadians intuitively understand why. What happens behind the border makes a fundamental difference to a strong social bond, vital public authority and dynamic practice of citizenship. Enough Canadians want to build a counterweight to American leadership, and disagreement with Washington is a legitimate expression of a democratic neighbour.

The overriding constant between the Republic and the

northern Confederation is that dominant social and political preferences are not easily set aside. North Americans are not unique in preferring their active localisms—far from it. The great French historian Ferdinand Braudel was also fascinated by the complex embedded plurality of French life and convinced that the local was the most central element of place and identity in shaping French unity. The final word must go to him: *"le singulier au sommet, le pluriel à la base"* [the singular at the summit, the plural at the base]. Place-rooted plurality and national diversity are the successors to national unity in Canada. In the end we are a continent of "strange multiplicities" demanding to be recognized but unable to share in the good life of our distinctive neighbouring society.

What is needed is the capacity to see beyond one's home and native land and to share with our neighbours what the late Stephen Jay Gould has termed in another connection, "the civic values of solace, solidarity and goodness in time of great need." A stunning example is this: after the Halifax explosion in 1917, Americans sent a hospital ship from Boston to treat Halifax's thousands of wounded and maimed. As an act of continuing gratitude and friendship, the city of Halifax sends a giant Christmas tree to the people of Boston each year to commemorate their kindness. It is these small gifts of human contact that in the end matter most. They are the substrata of a continent without a commonly recognized history and cannot be measured in commercial terms. Thoreau's idea of close "friends at a distance" is the right goal and creative ambiguity is the strategic calculus to position Canada in a new world order that presents itself as permanent, eternal and necessary. Politics as fate? The end of borders? A drop-dead convergence? Go figure.

# Appendix: Hinge Moments: A Short Chronology of the Canada-US Border and National Boundaries

## 1783

With the signing of the Treaty of Paris in 1783, North America is reorganized into discrete national entities with recognizable borders that delineate two very distinct societies with different political and social systems. With the exodus of more than one hundred thousand British loyalists, who travel north within less than a decade after the American War of Independence, the border represents a fixed geographical and natural point of demarcation.

## 1812

Since the American invasion in the war of 1812, Canada has not had to militarily defend its territory from its powerful neighbour. It leaves British North America exposed as "an imperial headland jutting out in a republican sea."

## 1846

Fixed by treaty in the East, the undefended 49th parallel border is extended westwards by the Oregon Treaty negotiated between Britain and the US. Provision is made to extend the border to the Pacific in 1866. This makes the Canada/US border one of the longest established and continuously recognized borders in the modern world. It has not moved a centimetre since, although there have been quarrels and conflicts over Alaska in 1903 and the Strait of Juan de Fuca, George's Strait and Arctic sovereignty in modern times.

## 1848

Through war and strong-arm diplomacy, the US seizes more than one-quarter of Mexico's territory and definitively establishes its southern border just two years after securing its northern border. Texas was annexed in 1845; this also included part of New Mexico and a very large finger of Colorado. California was "acquired" from Mexico by treaty in 1848, a vast territory that included Utah, Nevada, Arizona and California. When the United States Senate ratified the treaty, it erased Article 10, which guaranteed the protection of Mexican land grants; Article 9, which dealt with citizenship rights for Mexicans, was also weakened. In Texas, Mexicans were restricted from voting. By the end of the nineteenth century, most Mexicans in the American southwest had lost their land, either through force or fraud, or both. The land-hungry Americans concluded the Gadsden Purchase in 1853, giving them valuable territory in southern Arizona and what is now New Mexico. The new territory was key for the construction of the southern transcontinental railroad, which would connect western territories to the east and north. On the North American continent, American geopolitical power is unrivaled, as the US enters an age of unprecedented industrial growth, settlement and expansion.

## 1861–65

With the defeat of the Confederacy in the Civil War, the US republic emerges from the terrible slaughter of soldiers and civilians as "one and indivisible," but war-weary and bitterly divided by race, region and class. The celebrated American historian Fredrick Jackson Turner's 1893 account of the mythic frontier gains wide acceptance as it becomes equated with a self-confident rise in US cosmopolitanism. What Americans want to believe is that the "relentless moving frontier" represents the defining moment of American individualism and popular democracy.

## 1866

Washington, angered by British and Canadian support for the South, abruptly cancels the Reciprocity Treaty of 1854. American protectionism nurtures Canadian protectionism, but the national tariff policy later adopted by Macdonald and other politicians has the "perverse effect" of encouraging US investors and manufacturers to set up operations behind Canada's tariff wall. Many Maritime factories close, but Ontario's industries never look back and thrive. Ontario becomes the most heavily industrialized part of Canada.

## 1867

British elites believe that Canada's annexation is probably inevitable but are not ready to go to war with the US to keep Canada in the empire. With so little British interest in Canada, the momentum to create a new country is driven by popular sentiments for effective democracy, but only in part. The "quiet people of Canada" engineer Confederation, which passes in Westminister with as much interest, Sir John A. Macdonald complains, "as a private bill uniting two or three parishes." The new federal union makes English Canada supreme, recognizes Quebec only as a minority and gives wide powers to both the new federal government and the provinces. Canada's accomplishment in nation-building is flawed by its federal compromise and its part-Canadian, part-British nationality.

## 1900–14

Millions of people come to North America without travel and visa documents. Passport and travel papers are introduced post-1917 and are but one instance of growing state control over individuals.

## 1902

A quarter of Canadians born in Canada migrate to the US looking for work and employment. (By the 1990s only about 2 percent of Canadians born in Canada will live on the other side of the border, despite a century of economic integration.)

## 1905

With a uniquely stable land border, Canada as a new nation is far more busy with establishing its internal political boundaries. The Autonomy Act of 1905 expands western provincial boundaries, and in 1912 Ottawa extends the boundaries of the central provinces north. The US border remains a constant menace, as US business culture spills into Canada's national space, and Canada has yet to learn to assert itself to share the continent with the Republic.

## 1909

The Boundary Waters Treaty establishes the International Joint Commission, an independent binational entity charged to settle, through compromise and consensus, conflicts relating to the use and quality of water which had arisen between the two countries. It empowers Canadian and American bureaucrats and diplomats only to advise both governments on these and related questions. It deepens the conviction, particularly in Canada, that the Canada-US border is nonviolent and of low strategic order.

## 1914–17

Canadian nationhood and nation-building are forged in wartime. "[Canada's soldiers] went up Vimy Ridge as colonials and came down its bloody slopes as Canadians."

## 1932

R.B. Bennett, Canada's conservative, pro-business prime minister, establishes the Canadian Radio Broadcasting Commission, a publicly funded authority that guarantees Canadian citizens a democratic voice. In 1936 the Canadian Broadcasting Act replaces the CRBC with a Crown Corporation, the CBC. The CBC takes over CRBC staff and facilities (eight publicly owned or leased stations and fourteen private affiliates). The statute does not ban private broadcasting but forces wealthy private broadcasters to compete with a public authority possessing relatively few resources. By the late 1930s, new CBC transmitters in Toronto and Montreal dramatically increase national coverage from 49 percent to 76 percent of the population, in stiff competition from US sources.

## 1939

US authorities unilaterally demand that all Canadians entering the US have passports.

## 1940

The Ogdensburg Agreement, proposed by Roosevelt to King, represents a quantum leap in military cooperation between the two countries. The Permanent Defence Board is established and arrangements are formalized in the Hyde Park Declaration a year later. Some experts regard this "unalarming beginning" as the critical first step toward a doctrine of US Homeland Security.

## 1947

Only belatedly does Canada begin issuing Canadian passports to Canadian citizens. The National Citizenship Act is the first statute of substance that establishes domicile and naturalization through the immigration machinery of the state. It takes eighty years after Confederation before Canadian citizenship with a distinct legal identity separate from Britain is finally promulgated.

## 1947

The US passes the National Security Act with little debate. The Act creates the legislative machinery to establish highly autonomous intelligence agencies to defend US national interests from foreign power threat, with the minimal oversight of Congress. Conceived as a response to new dangers, it rationalized covert activities as a necessary, critical and permanent part of American security doctrine at home and abroad. It put the US state on a permanent footing, in the words of American historian Charles A. Beard, "to wage perpetual war for perpetual peace."

## 1947–48

Senior Canadian and US officials enter into secret free trade negotiations and conclude the draft outline of a pact. Mackenzie King gets cold feet and vetoes it. He does not believe that it can be sold to the Canadian electorate. Among other things, the pact has a term of twenty-five years and would not be subject to termination by either government until the end of the term and then only with three years' notice. It is a naive document, incomplete and foolishly conceived, and most advantageous to US vital interests.

## 1951

The Massey-Levesque Commission on Arts, Letters and Sciences warns Canadians that they are threatened by American culture, ideas and products. "Few Canadians realize the extent of this dependence." It is alarmed that Canadians take "more direction from New York than they would think of taking from Ottawa." It calls on Ottawa to provide state support for indigenous Canadian culture and "reverse the present danger of permanent dependence."

## 1957–62

The North American Defence Agreement (NORAD) is signed into law by Diefenbaker. The defence of North America is planned, staffed and financed by the US military with a symbolic Canadian presence. Subsequently, Diefenbaker negotiates and signs the Defence Production Sharing Agreement, further integrating the two countries' defence industries. Diefenbaker, rhetorically the populist and nationalist, but in practice a poor defender of Canadian sovereignty, is a tragic figure. Outmanoeuvred by the Kennedy administration, Diefenbaker does not accept that nuclear weapons are needed to defend North America, but his policies lack clarity and coherence. In the Cuban missile crisis of 1962, he initially refuses to put Canadian forces on full alert, but NORAD headquarters in Colorado, under orders from Kennedy, proceeds anyway.

## 1964–65

The single-leaf design is adopted by the Canadian House of Commons in December 1964 as Canada's new official flag and takes effect on February 15, 1965, after a long and often acrimonious debate. It turns out to be a keystone initiative of the new Pearson Liberal government. The Pearson government's commitment to social reform and economic nationalism is short-lived, but Walter Gordon, the nationalist Minister of Finance, gives the country a new sense of national purpose. Few of his economic policies are adopted, but he strikes a deep chord with Canadians. Canada is gripped not by its own nationalism but that of Quebec's and the Quiet Revolution. Under Trudeau, constitutional reform, national unity and expansion of the welfare state become the principal axes of Canadian domestic politics for the next forty years. Universal health care is the institutional capstone of these policies on both sides of the linguistic divide.

## 1965

Prime Minister Pearson, speaking at Temple University in Philadelphia, calls on President Johnson to suspend air strikes against Hanoi and asks Hanoi to moderate its policy. The next day Pearson is summoned to Camp David by Johnson, who grabs Pearson's lapels, shouting, "You pissed on my rug."

## 1965

The Canada-US Auto Pact, arguably the best state-to-state deal that Ottawa ever negotiated, guarantees Canadian assembly plants a secure share of the continental market. Canada has always relied on government initiatives and strategies to develop an international-scale economy. This bilateral deal is far superior to anything comparable found in NAFTA.

## 1982

The patriation of the Canadian Constitution and the passage into law of the Charter of Rights and Freedoms reconfigures Canada's political culture, although Quebec does not sign it, instead legislating its own charter. It makes Canadians rights-conscious, particularly in relation to vulnerable groups and individuals. Section 1 addresses rights for a democratic society and emphasizes citizen-state protection from the perspective of the citizen. The Charter reaches out to a broad range of communities, including women, official language minorities, multiculturalists and others. It not only makes government policies accountable to the Charter but gives Canadians both a citizens' constitution and a governmental constitution for a modern society. Its effects are pervasive and contradictory, but it is popularly received.

## 1985

The landmark Canadian Supreme Court *Singh Ruling* requires the federal government to provide written reports of all refugee and immigration determination hearings. This decision by Madame Berthe Wilson accords immigrants and refugees full protection under the Canadian Charter of Rights and Freedoms. No refugee claimant can be removed based on an oral hearing before an immigration board.

## 1987

Mulroney and Reagan sign the Canada-US Free Trade Agreement, which accelerates economic integration. But without a definition of a subsidy in the text, Canada is afforded no protection from US trade law. Nor is there any commitment to positive integration that binds the US to build a North American community and pool its sovereignty for common ends. This option is not part of the FTA's framework and is explicitly rejected by Washington and the Congress.

## 1988

The Multiculturalism and Citizenship Act commits the federal government to protect ethnic diversity, ensure equal employment opportunities in federal institutions and establish policies and programs to develop active citizens. Section 27 of the Charter of Rights and Freedoms instructs judges to interpret the Charter "consistent with the preservation and enhancement of the multi-cultural heritage of Canadians." Global immigration flows into Canada break all records and transform Canada into a diverse multicultural society. Section 6 of the Charter protects the rights of all Canadians to enter and leave Canada without discrimination. A naturalized Canadian is to be treated no differently than a native-born.

## 1994

NAFTA comes into effect, establishing a free trade zone between Canada, Mexico and the US. Still, the border continues to generate huge revenues in taxes, duties and fees. In 1999, revenues from all fees, including the GST and PST, totalled more than $22 billion. There is no Niagara of people moving across the "open" border post-NAFTA, and no evidence of an incipient North American community emerging.

## 1994–97

Chrétien is elected and in the next three budgets federal spending for social programs is cut by about 20 percent. Public spending falls to record low levels. Still, for the period 1974–97, the inequalities among regions within each country are smaller than those between the two neighbours.

## 1995

With the narrow defeat of Quebec's referendum for independence, the Quebec nationalist project looses direction and political will. Charter activism propels citizenship and identity issues onto the public agenda.

## 1996

Clinton terminates the Aid to Families with Dependent Children, a pillar of the US welfare system, and replaces it with the highly restrictive Personal Responsibility and Work Opportunities Reconciliation Act. For the first time a sharp distinction is drawn between the citizen and the immigrant, and the deserving and undeserving citizen. Almost two million Americans are removed from the welfare roles. The Congress also passes the Illegal Immigration Reform and Immigrant Act as the US begins to closely monitor and control the cross-border movement of all non-US citizens, including Canadians and Mexicans.

## 2000

US Supreme Court intervention in the Florida electoral recount supports Bush and effectively declares him president.

## 2001

9/11 terrorist attacks on World Trade Centre and the Pentagon. Canada and the US sign the Smart Border Accord, an initiative begun by the Clinton and Chrétien governments. It is an action plan "to ensure the flow of goods, people, infrastructure and sharing" continent-wide but is subject to the far-reaching power of both the 2001 US Patriot and Homeland Security Acts.

## 2001–2

Canada establishes mirror legislation to conform to many of the assumptions and goals of homeland security, passing in record time the Immigration and Refugee Protection Act and the Anti-Terrorism Act, giving Ottawa and police agencies new powers to deport, detain and prosecute citizens and non-citizens based on police suspicion of their ethnic background and association with immigrant communities.

## 2002

The Homeland Security Act, which establishes the US Department of Homeland Security, represents the largest governmental reorganization in the US in fifty years and defines the border as "everywhere and everything." The US Bio-terrorism Act imposes new rules and regulations regarding all shipments of food to the US, with pre-inspection of food products made mandatory.

## 2004

The security-first border requires all visitors to the US to register and be finger-printed by US immigration and intelligence authorities. The transformation of the commerce-first border into a security-first border is to be complete by 2006. More screening, scanning and surveillance of passengers, visitors, students, tourists, immigrants, vehicles, containers, food parcels and shipments of every kind are projected and in the final stages of implementation.

# ENDNOTES

## Preface

1.  Denis Stairs, "Canada in the Post-9/11 World: Old Perceptions and New Realities." *Canadian Issues* (Summer 2000).
2.  George Hoberg, Keith Banting and Richard Simeon, "The Scope for Domestic Policy Choice: Policy Autonomy in a Globalizing World," in George Hoberg, ed., *Capacity for Choice: Canada in the New North America* (Toronto: University of Toronto, 2003) p. 269.
3.  Louis Pauly, "Canada-U.S. Economic Relations," Munk Centre, University of Toronto, from Global Market Information Database, March 2003, p. 2.
4.  Thomas L. Friedman, *The Lexus and the Olive Tree: Understanding Globalization* (New York: Farrar Straus Giroux, 1999).
5.  Earl Fry and Jared Bybee, "NAFTA 2002: A cost/benefit analysis for the United States, Canada and Mexico," *Canadian-American Public Policy*, no. 49, (January 2002) p. 8 and 5.
6.  Keith Banting, George Hoberg and Richard Simeon, eds., *Degrees of Freedom: Canada and the United States in a Changing World* (Montreal: McGill-Queen's, 1997).

## Chapter 1

1.  Engin Isin, *Being Political: Genealogies of Citizenship* (Minneapolis: University of Minnesota Press, 2002) p. 30.
2.  Gore Vidal, *Dreaming War: Blood for Oil and the Cheney-Bush Junta* (New York: Thunder's Mouth Press/Nations Books, 2002).
3.  Homeland Security Act of 2002: <http://news.findlaw.com/wp/docs/terrorism/hsa2002.pdf>
4.  Bruce Hutchinson, quoted in Lorraine Monk, ed., *Between Friends/Entre Amis* (Toronto: McClelland and Stewart, 1976) p. 69.
5.  Paul Koring, "Crisis in Iraq: US sticks to its guns in UN rift: Countdown to war: Powell brushes off Blix and European allies, saying US can go it alone," *Globe and Mail*, March 6, 2003.
6.  Homeland Security Act.

7.  *Our Shared Border: Facilitating the Movement of Goods and People in a Security Environment*, House of Commons Standing Committee on Banking, Trade and Commerce, Interim Report, Chair Hon. Leo Kolber (Ottawa, 2002) p. 4.

8.  William Paley, "Resources for Freedom: A Report to the President by the President's Materials Policy Commission." Washington, D.C., 1952.

9.  Patriot Act of 2001. <http://news.findlaw.com/hdocs/docs/terrorism/hr3162.pdf>

10.  Jeff Fogel, *The State of Civil Liberties: One Year Later Erosion of Civil Liberties in the Post 9/11 Era,* Centre for Constitutional Rights (Washington, D.C., 2002). <www.ccr-ny.org/v2/reports/report.asp?ObjID=keheMUpDud&Content=285>

11.  Heather Segal, "Welcome to the border," *Globe and Mail,* March 7, 2003.

12.  Bioterrorism Act of 2002. <www.fda.gov/oc/bioterrorism/bioact.html>

13.  David Grossman, "The Arar case should scare us all: Canadian citizen detained in Syria 10 months for alleged terrorist ties," *Globe and Mail*, September 12, 2003.

14.  Audrey Macklin, "Mr. Easter, we need a probe of the Arar Case," *Globe and Mail*, November 14, 2003.

15.  Audrey Macklin, *Borderline Security*, Public Law and Legal Theory Research Paper no. 02-3 (University of Toronto, 2002).

16.  Safe Third Country Agreement of 2002, Citizenship and Immigration Canada (Ottawa, 2002). <www.cic.gc.ca/english/policy/safe-third.html>

17.  Jeff Salot, "Famed Syrian lawyer to act for Canadian," *Globe and Mail,* September 19, 2003.

18.  Greg Keenan, "Windsor-Detroit border: Road rage for auto makers," *Globe and Mail,* March 8, 2003.

19.  Paul Koring, "Crisis in Iraq: President readies for war; US president takes his message to a prime-time television audience on eve of pivotal UN meeting," *Globe and Mail*, March 7, 2003.

20.  Frank Griffiths, "The shipping news: Canada's Arctic sovereignty not on thinning ice," *International Journal* 58, no. 2 (Spring 2003).

21.  Margaret Macmillan, *Paris 1919: Six Months That Changed the World* (New York: Random House, 2001).

22.  Industry Canada, *Canada's Growing Economic Relations with the United States* (Ottawa, 2002), p. L-4.

23.  Andrew Cooper, *Canadian Foreign Policy: Old Habits and New Directions* (Scarborough, Ont: Prentice-Hall Allyn and Bacon Canada, 1997).

24.  Clyde Prestowitz, *Rogue Nation: American Unilateralism and the*

*Failure of Good Intentions* (New York: Basic Books, 2003).

25. Quoted in Robert Skidelsky, *John Maynard Keynes,* vol. III, (London: Macmillan, 2000), p. 373.

26. Denis Stairs, "Canada in the post-9/11 World: Old Perceptions and New Realities," *Canadian Issues* (Summer 2000).

27. Andrew Cooper, "Waiting at the Perimeter: Making US Policy in Canada," in Maureen Appel Molot and Fen Osler Hampton, eds., *Canada Among Nations 2000: Vanishing Borders* (Don Mills, Ont.: Oxford University Press, 2000).

28. Michael Hardt and Antonio Negri, *Empire* (Cambridge: Harvard University Press, 2000), p. 11.

29. Robert Cox, "Beyond Empire and Terror: Critical Reflections on the Political Economy of World Order," lecture given at the University of Sheffield, November 2003. <www.shef.ac.uk/~perc/lectures/cox.pdf>

30. Robert Kagan, *Of Paradise and Power: America and Europe in the New World Order* (New York: Knopf, 2003), p. 27.

31. *Financial Times,* September 19, 2003.

32. Personal communication with Deputy Minister of Canada Customs and Revenue, June 15, 2001. Canada Customs accounting document 3, 1999/2000.

33. For a less technical review of the issues, see John Helliwell, *Globalization and Well-Being* (Vancouver: UBC, 2002); Michael Adams' new study of Canada-US relations, *Fire and Ice: The United States, Canada and the Myth of Inevitability* (Toronto: Penguin, 2003). Also see *Canada Watch, Special Issue, Canada-US Relations* 8: 4–5, November–December 2002, available at <www.robarts.yorku.ca>

34. John McCallum, "National Borders Matter: Canada-US Regional Trade Patterns," *American Economic Review* 85 (June 1995): p. 615–23; John F. Helliwell, *How Much Do Borders Matter?* (Washington, D.C.: Brookings Institution, 1998).

35. Helliwell, ibid., p. 4.

36. John F. Helliwell and Ross McKitrick, "Comparing Capital Mobility across Provincial and National Borders," *Canadian Journal of Economics* 32, no. 5 (November 1999), p. 1166.

37. Bruce Little, "Romanow Report: But elixir will erase surpluses through to 2006" *Globe and Mail,* November 29, 2002; and "Medicare: Fixing the health system: When looking at healthcare, best to follow the money! Figures reveal much about the cost of system, shifts in spending patterns over the years," *Globe and Mail,* November 27, 2002

38. Ronald Kneebone and Kenneth McKenzie, *Past (In)Discretions Canada: Federal and Provincial Fiscal Policy* (Toronto: University of Toronto, 1999), p. 47.

39. Ibid.
40. The numbers are cited by John Ibbitson in his *Globe and Mail* column, August 15, 2002, and are from an OECD study, Paris, 2002.
41. Andrew Jackson, "Poverty and Income Inequality in the 1990s," *Economy* 13, no. 3 (Winter 2002–3), CLC, Ottawa.
42. George Hoberg, Keith Banting and Richard Simeon, "The Scope for Domestic Policy Choice: Policy Autonomy in a Globalizing World," in George Hoberg, ed., *Capacity for Choice: Canada in the New North America* (Toronto: University of Toronto, 2003), p. 269.
43. Paul T. Mitchell, Canadian Forces College, "A Transformation Agenda for the Canadian Forces: Full Spectrum Influence," forthcoming in the proceedings of Dalhousie University's 2003 "Seapower" conference.

## Chapter 2

1. Personal communication, Daniel Latouche.
2. Margaret Macmillan, *Paris 1919: Six Months That Changed the World* (New York: Random House, 2001).
3. US Immigration and Naturalization Services, 2002 <www.ins.usdoj.gov/graphics/aboutins/statistics/msrsep01/REMOVAL.HTM>
4. Tapen Sinha, "Three's Company: US Borders after September 11," *Texas Business Review* (February 2002), Bureau of Business Research, McCombs School of Business, University of Texas at Austin.
5. Theodore H. Cohen, "Cross Border Travel in North America: The Challenge of US Section 110 Legislation," *Canadian-American Public Policy*, no. 40 (October 1999).
6. *Financial Times*, February 8/9, 2003.
7. Bernard Lewis, *What Went Wrong? The Clash between Islam and Modernity in the Middle East* (New York, Harper Collins, 2002).
8. John Keegan, *The First World War* (New York: Vintage, 2000), p. 175.
9. John Torpey, *The Invention of the Passport: Surveillance, Citizenship and the State* (London: Cambridge University Press, 2000), p. 20.
10. <www.ppt.gc.ca/passport_office/history_e.asp>
11. Martin Shaw, *Theory of the Global State: Globality as an Unfinished Revolution* (London: Cambridge University Press, 2000).
12. Dava Sobel and William J.H. Andewres, *The Illustrated Longitude: The True Story of a Lone Genius Who Solved the Greatest Scientific Problem of His Time* (Toronto: Penguin, 2003).
13. Alan Moorhead, *The White Nile* (London: Penguin Books, 1960) p. 340–41.
14. Norman Nicholson, *The Boundaries of the Canadian Federation* (Toronto: Macmillan Canada, Carleton Library, 1979).
15. Ibid., p. 162 and 170.

16. Ibid., p. 8.
17. Ibid., p. 14.
18. On the importance of the map, national census statistics and the museum as instruments of nationhood, see Benedict Anderson's highly influential *Imagined Communities: Reflections on the Origins and Spread of Nationalism* (London: Verso, 1983).
19. D.W. Meinig, *The Shaping of America*, vol. 1 (New Haven: Yale University Press, 1986).
20. Derek Hayes, *Historical Atlas of Canada: Canada's History Illustrated with Original Maps* (Toronto/Vancouver: Douglas & McIntyre, 2002).
21. Thomas Wilson and Hastings Donnan, *Border Identities: Nation and State at International Frontiers* (Cambridge: Cambridge University Press, 1998), p. 7.
22. John Herd Thompson and Stephen Randall, *Canada and the United States: Ambivalent Allies* second ed., (Athens and London: University of Georgia Press, 1997).
23. H.V. Nelles, *The Politics of Development* (Toronto: Macmillan, 1974).
24. His diary is available online at <http://king.archives.ca>
25. David Haglund, "North American Isolationism," *International Journal* 58, no. 2 (Winter 2003), p. 13.
26. Hugh Keenleyside, from *Canada and the United States* (1929), quoted in Lorraine Monk, ed., *Between Friends/Entre Amis* (Toronto: McClelland and Stewart, 1976), p. 4.
27. Francis M. Carroll, *A Good and Wise Measure: The Search for the Canadian-American Boundary, 1783–1842* (Toronto: University of Toronto Press, 2001).
28. Bruce Hutchinson, quoted in Monk, *Between Friends/Entre Amis*, p. 69.
29. Nicholson, *The Boundaries of the Canadian Federation*.
30. Daniel Drache, ed., *Staples, Markets and Cultural Change: The Centenary Edition of the Collected Essays of Harold Innis* (Montreal: McGill-Queens, 1995).
31. D.W. Meinig, "Symbolic Landscapes: Some Idealizations of American Communities," in John Brinckerhoff Jackson and Donald William Meinig, eds., *The Interpretation of Ordinary Landscapes: Geographical Essays* (New York: Oxford University Press, 1979), p. 143.
32. Quoted in Lorne Pierce, *An Editor's Creed* (Toronto: Ryerson Press. 1960), p. 2.
33. David James Smith, "Intellectual Activist: Graham Spry, A Biography," Ph.D. dissertation, Department of History, York University, September 2002, p. 248.
34. Pre 9/11, nationals from countries who are part of the US visa waiver program did not need to obtain a visa for each visit. Upon filling out the visa waiver, the individual's name was entered in the US immigra-

tion system and in theory could be permanently tracked and monitored. The monitoring was haphazard and hundreds of thousands of
visa holders overstayed their visits and remained in the US. Argentina
was recently kicked out of the program because too many Argentin-
ians were overstaying their residency conditions.

35. US Department of Justice, Immigration and Naturalization Service,
OMB no.1115-0148, I-94W Non-immigrant Visa Waiver Arrival/De-
parture Form that every non-immigrant visitor to the US has to fill out.
The countries participating in this program are listed in 8 CFR 217.

36. D.W. Meinig, *Shaping of America*.

37. Ibid., p. 417.

38. Henry Nash Smith, *Virgin Land: The American West as Symbol and
Myth* (Cambridge, Mass.: Harvard University Press, 1950), p. 293.

39. Michael Bliss, "Canadianizing American Business: The Roots of the
Branch Plant," in C.I. Lumsden, ed., *Close the 49th Parallel Etc.*
(Toronto: University of Toronto, 1970).

40. For a review of who's who in Canadian history, see Carl Berger, *The
Writing of Canadian History* (Toronto: Oxford University Press, 1976).
For an important re-examination, see Marlene Shore, "'Remember
the Future': The *Canadian Historical Review* and the Discipline of
History, 1920–95," *Canadian Historical Review* 76, no. 3 (September
1995). Her thesis is compelling—as Canadian History evolves, so goes
the nation!

41. Daniel Drache, "Goals and Values Inescapably Public," in Daniel
Drache, ed., *The Market or the Public Domain: Global Governance
and the Asymmetry of Power* (London: Routledge, 2001).

42. D.W. Meinig, "The Beholding Eye: Ten Versions of the Same Scene,"
in J.B. Jackson and D.W. Meinig, eds., *The Interpretation of Ordinary
Landscapes*, p. 42.

43. Stephen Pearlstein, *Washington Post,* September 5, 2000.

44. Lansing Lamont began his 1994 book, *Breakup: The Coming End of
Canada and the Stakes for America,* (New York: Norton), with the
following provocative sentence: "Nations like stars burn out.... Maybe
Canada is not meant to survive. Maybe it isn't destined to live out its
span as a nation."

45. Quoted in William Robbins, *Colony and Empire: The Capitalist
Transformation of the American West* (Lawrence: University of Kansas,
1994), p. 53.

46. Kerwin Lee Klein, *Frontiers of Historical Imagination* (Berkeley: University of California Press, 1997), p. 208.

47. Ken Coates, "Border Crossings: Patterns and Processes Along the
Canada–United States Boundary West of the Rockies," in Ken Coates
and John M. Finlay, eds., *Parallel Destinies* (Montreal: McGill Queen's,
2003).

48. Kim Lunman, "War in Iraq: The homefront: War strains goodwill in small border town: Ottawa decision not to back coalition feels like slapping a friend in the face, Vermonter says," *Globe and Mail*, March 31, 2003.

49. James Macdonald, *The North American Idea* (Toronto: McClelland, Goodchild and Stewart, 1917), p. 69.

50. Ibid., p. 69 and 74.

## Chapter 3

1. Michael Adams, *Fire and Ice* (Toronto: Penguin, 2003).

2. John Helliwell, *Globalization: Myths, Facts and Consequences* Benefactors Lecture, C.D. Howe Institute, 2000.

3. Canadian Immigration (Ottawa, 2002).

4. Louis Pauly, "Canada-US Economic Relations," Munk Centre, University of Toronto, 2003, unpublished.

5. Drew Fagan, "Working for the Yankee dollar—Like it or not!" *Globe and Mail*, March 8, 2003.

6. Don Drummond, Chief economist of TD Financial Bank Group, "Canada and the Global Economy," (Toronto: TD Financial Bank Group, January 18, 2001).

7. Some Canadian companies have responded to the NAFTA challenge by pretending to be a US company. CCL, one of North America's largest packaging companies, reported that American firms were reluctant "to deal with Canadian customers, so we moved our divisional office to Chicago," according to its president and founder. His idea was to hide the fact that CCL was Canadian and pass itself off as a US firm. See Oliver Bertin, *Globe and Mail*, April 19, 2003.

8. See Daniel Drache et al., "WTO and Social Diversity: Second WTO Report Card on Trade and Social Inclusion," 2001. <www.robarts.yorku.ca>

9. Eric Helleiner, "Towards a North American Currency," in Wallace Clement and Leah Vosko, eds., *Changing Canada: Political Economy as Transformation* (Montreal: McGill-Queen's, 2003).

10. Paul Krugman, *Geography and Trade* (Boston: M.I.T. Press, 1991), p. 26.

11. Ibid.

12. Ontario and Nuevo Leon in Mexico play similar hub-spoke roles in their respective economies. See Isidro Morales, "NAFTA: The Institutionalization of Economic Openness and the Configuration of Mexican Geo-Economic Spaces," *Third World Quarterly* 20, no. 5 (1999).

13. "Who Pays? A Distributional Analysis of the Tax Systems in all 50 States," second ed. (Washington, D.C.: Institute on Taxation and Economic Policy, January 2003). <www.itepnet.org>

14. Timothy Smeeding, Lee Rainwater and Gary Burtless, "United States Poverty in Cross-National Context," draft paper prepared for the IRP conference volume, *Understanding Poverty in America: Progress and Problems*, September 28, 2000, p. 11.

15. Kerwin Lee Klein, *Frontiers of Historical Imagination* (Berkeley: University of California Press, 1997).

16. Ibid.

17. D.W. Meinig, "Continental America, 1800–1915: The View of an Historical Georgrapher," *The History Teacher* 22, no. 2 (February 1989).

18. Marshall McLuhan, "Canada: The Borderline Case," in David Staines, ed., *The Canadian Imagination: Dimensions of a Literary Culture* (Cambridge, Mass.: Harvard University Press, 1977), p. 234.

19. Harold Innis, *Staples, Markets and Cultural Change: Selected Essays*, ed. by Daniel Drache (Montreal: McGill-Queen's, 1995), p. xvii.

20. Bruce Little, "Mayors, business should team up on infrastructure," *Globe and Mail*, November 24, 2003.

21. Irene Bloemraad, "Whither Canadian Multiculturalism?" memo prepared for "On the Edge: Is the Canadian Model Sustainable?" Harvard University, Mackenzie King conference, Weatherhead Centre for International Affairs, May 9–10, 2003.

22. See <http://www.pch.gc.ca/progs/multi/reports/ann97-98/public_e.cfm> Multiculuralism Act: Canadian Multiculturalism Act R.S., 1985, c. 24 (4th Supp.), An Act for the preservation and enhancement of multiculturalism in Canada [*1988, c. 31, assented to 21st July, 1988*]. To consult the whole act, go to <http://www.canlii.org/ca/sta/c-18.7/whole.html>

23. Bloemraad, "Whither Canadian Multiculturalism?"

24. Danielle Juteau, "The Citizen Makes an Entrée: Redefining the National Community in Quebec," *Citizenship Studies* 6, no. 4 (2002).

25. Statistics Canada, "Canada's Ethnocultural Portrait: The Changing Mosaic" (Ottawa: Statistics Canada, 2003). <www.statscan.ca>

26. See Eric Anderssen's feature article on Fahima Osman, the first Canadian-trained physican from Toronto's Somali community, *Globe and Mail*, June 14, 2003.

27. *Globe and Mail*, June 14, 2003, F5.

28. Bloemraad, "Whither Canadian Multiculturalism?"

29. R. Kent Weaver, *Ending Welfare As We Know It* (Washington: Brookings Institution, 2000).

30. Michael Fix and Jeffery Passel, *The Scope and Impact of Welfare Reform's Immigrant Provisions, Assessing the New Federalism* (Washington, D.C.: Urban Institute, January 2002).

31. Alexander Aleinikoff and Douglas Lusmeyer, *Social Rights and Citizenship* (Washington, D.C.: Carnegie Endowment for International Peace,

2002), p. 67.

32. Weaver, *Ending Welfare As We Know It.*

33. June O'Neill and M. Anne Hill, *Gaining Ground? Measuring the Impact of Welfare Reform on Welfare and Work* (New York: Centre for Civic Innovation at the Manhattan Institute, July 2001), Civic Report no. 17, Figure 1, p. 4.

34. Alice Rivlin, *Another State Fiscal Crisis: There Must be a Better Way* (Washington, D.C.: Brookings Institution, October 15, 2002).

35. National Governors Association, *Fiscal Survey of States* (Washington, D.C.: May 2002). <www.nga.org>

36. Rivlin, *Another State Fiscal Crisis.*

37. Nicholas Lemann, "The Mark of Karl Rove," *New Yorker,* May 12, 2003, p. 83.

38. Ibid.

39. Hershel Hardin, *A Nation Unaware: The Canadian Economic Culture* (Vancouver: J.J. Douglas, 1974).

40. Suzanne Kennedy and Steven Gonzalez, "Government Spending in Canada and the US," Working Paper 2003-05 (Ottawa: Department of Finance).

41. M. Wolfson and B. Murphy, "Income Inequality in North America: Does the 49th Parallel Still Matter?" *Canadian Economic Observer* (August 2000), Statistics Canada, p. 3.21.

42. Ibid., p. 3.12.

43. Paul Krugman, "For Richer," *New York Times,* October 20, 2002.

44. Stephen Blank, *The United States on the Eve of the 21st Century,* Global Business Policy Council, Policy Briefing no. 7, April 1994.

45. Sylvia Bashevkin, "Rethinking Retrenchment: North American Social Policy during the Early Clinton and Chrétien Years," *Canadian Journal of Political Science* 33, no. 1 (March 2000).

46. Gerard Boychuk and Keith Banting, "The Paradox of Convergence: National Versus Sub-National Patterns of Convergence in Canadian and American Income Maintenance Policy," prepared for Industry Canada's "North American Linkages Project: Opportunities and Challenges for Canada," submitted September 2001, p. 3.

47. Shawn McCarthy, "Prime Minister and Bush 'chit-chat' after months of tension," *Globe & Mail,* June 2, 2003.

48. Daniel Drache and Andrew Ranachan, *Warm Heart, Cold Country: Fiscal and Social Policy Reform in Canada* (Ottawa: Caledon Institute, 1995).

49. The figures were put together by Andrew Jackson when he was the chief researcher at the Canadian Council on Social Development in 2002. His full report can be accessed at <www.ccsd.ca/pubs/2002/olympic/indicators.htm>.

Chapter 4

1. Alain Noel, "Is Centralization Conservative? Federalism and the Contemporary Debate on the Canadian Welfare State," in Robert Young, ed., *Stretching the Federation: The Art of the State in Canada* (Kingston, Ont.: Institute of Intergovernmental Relations, Queen's University, 1999).

2. Stephen Clarkson, "Fearful Asymmetries: The Challenge of Analyzing Continental Systems in a Globalizing World," *Canadian-American Public Policy*, no. 35 (September 1998), p. 55.

3. Andrew Gamble, *Politics and Fate* (London: Polity Press, 2000).

4. Quoted from Daniel Drache, "The return of the public domain after the triumph of markets," in Daniel Drache, ed., *The Market or the Public Domain: Global Governance and the Asymmetry of Power* (London: Routledge, 2002).

5. Earl Fry and Jared Bybee, "NAFTA 2002: A cost/benefit analysis for the United States, Canada and Mexico," *Canadian-American Public Policy* 49 (January 2002), p. 5.

6. Perrin Beatty, "North American Partnership Inevitable," *National Post*, September 12, 2002.

7. John Helliwell, "Globalization: Myths, Facts and Consequences," Benefactors Lecture 2000, C.D. Howe Institute, Toronto.

8. Nora Lustig, "Life Is Not Easy: Mexico's Quest for Stability and Growth," *Journal of Economic Perspectives* 15, no. 1 (Winter 2001).

9. Ibid., p. 102.

10. Quentin Wodon and Norman Hicks, "Protecting the Poor during Crisis through Public Spending? Framework and Application to Argentina and Mexico," (Washington, D.C.: World Bank, Poverty and Reduction and Economic Management Network, 1999), quoted by Lustig, "Life Is Not Easy."

11. Lustig, "Life Is Not Easy," p. 103.

12. Raul Hinojosa, David Runsten, Freando De Paolis and Nabil Kamel, "The U.S. Employment Impacts of NAFTA: A Partial Equilibrium Approach" (Los Angeles: North American Integration and Development Centre School of Public Policy and Social Research, UCLA, January 2000). <http://naid.sppr.ucla.edu>

13. Tapen Sinha and Bradly Condon, "Three's Company, US Borders After September 11," *Texas Business Review*, University of Texas at Austin (February 2002).

14. Isidro Morales, "The Governance of Global Issues through Regionalism," November 2002, unpublished paper, UDLA, Puebla Mexico.

15. George Grant, "In Defence of North America," *Technology and Empire: Perspectives on North America* (Toronto: Anansi, 1969).

16. Kent Weaver, *Ending Welfare as We Know It* (Washington, D.C.:

Brookings Institution, 2000); Ken Battle, *Minimum Wages in Canada: A Statistical Portrait with Policy Implications* (Ottawa: Caledon Institute, 2003).

17. Bruno Theret, *Protection sociale et fédéralisme L'Europe dans le miroir de l'Amerique du Nord* (Paris: PUM, 2003); Keith Banting, George Hoberg and Richard Simeon, eds., *Degrees of Freedom: Canada and the United States in a Changing World* (Montreal: McGill-Queen's, 1997).

18. Michael Trebilcock, *Trade Liberalization, Regulatory Diversity and Political Sovereignty* (Toronto: Faculty of Law, University of Toronto, November 2003).

19. Daniel Drache, "Happy Fifth Birthday, NAFTA: Thinking Outside the Box, A Report on NAFTA Effects," 1999. <www.robarts.yorku.ca>

20. The details of the Mexico-US sugar dispute is summarized by Gustavo Vega Canovas in "The Role of NAFTA Dispute Settlement in the Management of Canadian, Mexican and US Trade and Investment Relations," February 2003, El Colegio de Mexico.

21. "Rules put pressure on Mexican trucking," *Financial Times,* December 5, 2002.

22. "Tuna dispute runs deeper than the death of dolphins," *Financial Times*, June 23, 2003.

23. The contrast with the European Union is noteworthy. The EU reserved the right to protect its health, education and audio-visual services in the Doha Developmental Round and intends to develop the necessary regulatory framework to protect is public services. See <http://europa.eu.int/comm/trade/services/pr050203_en.htm>.

24. Steven Shrybman, "Water Export Controls and Canadian International Trade Obligations: A Legal Opinion" (Vancouver, B.C.: West Coast Environmental Law Association, 1999). <www.wcel.org>

25. Scott Sinclair, "NAFTA Trade Disputes Update," compiled by the Trade and Investment Research Project, (Ottawa: CCPA, March 2003).

26. For an incisive analysis of NAFTA's legal culture, see Barry Appleton, *Navigating nafta: A Concise User's Guide to the North American Free Trade Agreement* (Toronto: Carswell, 1994); and Michael Trebilcock and Robert Howse, *The Regulation of International Trade,* second edition, (London: Routledge, 1999).

27. C. Lipson, *Standing Guard: Protecting Foreign Capital in the Nineteenth and Twentieth Centuries* (Berkeley: University of California Press, 1985).

28. J. Anthony VanDuzer, *NAFTA Chapter 11 to Date: The Progress of a Work in Progress* (Ottawa: DFAIT, 2002); Jim Stanford, "The North American Free Trade Agreement: Context, Structure, and Performance," in Jonathan Michie, ed., *The Handbook of Globalisation* (London: University of London, 2003).

29. Morales, "Governance of Global Issues Through Regionalism."
30. Quoted in Robert L. Earle and John Wirth, eds., *Identities in North America* (Palo Alto: Stanford University Press, 1995), p. 267.
31. Industry Canada, "Canada's Growing Economic Relations with the United States, Part 1: What Are the Key Dimensions?" *Micro-Economic Monitor*, Ottawa, (2001), p. M2.
32. Marjorie Cohen, "From Public Good to Private Exploitation: GATS and the Restructuring of Canadian Electrical Utilities," *Canadian-American Public Policy* no. 48 (2001).
33. David Elkins, *Beyond Sovereignty: Territory and Political Economy in the Twenty-First Century* (Toronto: University of Toronto Press, 1995), p. 78.
34. Canadians and Americans share a concern for localism with Europeans and many Latin American countries as well, as David Robinson underlines in his insightful essay, "The language and significance of place in Latin America," in John A. Agnew and James S. Duncan, eds., *The Power of Place* (Boston: Unwin Hyman, 1989).
35. Carnegie Foundation, *Caught in the Middle: Communities in an Era of Globalization* (Washington, D.C.: Carnegie Foundation, 2001).
36. Michael Adams, *Fire and Ice* (Toronto: Penguin, 2003), p. 50.
37. The high standard of transparency and participation adopted by the Aahaus Convention in 2001 could well serve as a benchmark for developing North America as a social entity beyond the market. It is based on principle 10 of the Rio Conference on Environment and Development in 1998 by the Fourth Ministerial Conference of the "Environment for Europe process" and entered into force in 2001 with forty signatories. See Sylvia Ostry, "What are the Necessary Ingredients for the World Trading Order?" paper prepared for the Kiel Institute of World Economics, June 2002.

## Chapter 5

1. Jeffrey Simpson, "Worried about US retribution? Don't be," *Globe and Mail*, April 9, 2003, B1.
2. Homeland Security Act of 2002. <http://news.findlaw.com/wp/docs/terrorism/hsa2002.pdf>
3. Public Health Security and Bioterrorism Preparedness and Response Act of 2002. <www.aphis.usda.gov/vs/ncie/pdf/bioterrorism_final.pdf>
4. Frank J. Murray, "Patriot Act of 2001 casts wide net," *Washington Times*, June 16, 2003.
5. Executive summary of HR 5710, Homeland Security Act of 2002. <http://www.whitehouse.gov/homeland/book/index.html>
6. Andrew Cooper, "Waiting at the Perimeter: Making US Policy in

Canada," in Maureen Appel Molot and Fen Osler Hampson, eds., *Canada among Nations, 2000: Vanishing Borders* (Don Mills: Oxford University Press, 2000).

7.  Philip Bobbitt, *The Shield of Achilles: War, Peace and the Course of History* (New York: Alfred Knopf, 2002).

8.  Daniel Drache and Marc Froese, "Poverty Eradication and the WTO," Robarts Centre for Canadian Studies, September 2003. <www.robarts.yorku.ca>

9.  As reported in the *Financial Times*, November 26, 2002, agricultural tariffs have clouded US-Mexico talks.

10. The INS is now the Bureau of Citizenship and Immigration Services (BCIS), a bureau of the US Department of Homeland Security, and is found at <www.immigration.gov>, where the number of removals are listed.

11. Heather Segal, "Welcome to the Border," *Globe and Mail*, March 7, 2003.

12. Victor Mallek, *"Is your passport worth the paper?" Globe and Mail*, March 15, 2003.

13. Canadian Immigration and Refugee Board (CIRB), 2002. Also see Margaret Philp, "Pakistanis flocking to Canada," *Globe and Mail*, March 15, 2003.

14. <www.whitehouse.gov/news/releases/2002/07/20020716.html>

15. CNN, March 15, 2003, Saturday Weekend News.

16. *Toronto Star,* March 10, 2003.

17. Theodore H. Cohen, "Cross Border Travel in North America: The Challenge of US Section 110 Legislation," *Canadian-American Public Policy* no. 40 (October 1999), p. 3.

18. Michael Fix and Jeffery Passel, "The Scope and Impact of Welfare Reform's Immigrant Provisions," Discussion Paper, 02-03, *Assessing the New Federalism* (Washington, D.C.:Urban Institute, 2002).

19. Carnegie Foundation, *Caught in the Middle: Communities in an Era of Globalization* (Washington, D.C.: Carnegie Foundation, 2001).

20. Chris Hedges, *War Is a Force That Gives Us Meaning* (New York: Anchor Books, 2003), p. 13.

21. Stephen Krasner, "Think Again: Sovereignty," *Foreign Policy* no. 122 (January/February 2001).

22. John Keane, *Global Civil Society?* (London: Cambridge University Press, 2003), p. 22.

23. Saskia Sassen, "Beyond Sovereignty: Immigration Policy Making Today," *Social Justice* 23 no. 3 (Fall 1996).

24. John Torpey, *The Invention of the Passport: Surveillance, Citizenship and the State* (London: Cambridge University Press, 2000).

25. The data are from the US Committee on Refugees at <http://www.refugees.org/world/articles/wrs02_easial.cfm#japan>.

26. Robert Howse, "Special Symposium: Boundaries of the WTO," *American Journal of International Law* 96 (2002).

27. Despite large gaps in the rules and frequent disregard of international norms by many states, international human rights advocates remain cautiously optimistic with the establishment of the International War Crimes Court.

28. For details on its mandate, see <http://www.un.org/law/icc/general/overview.htm>.

29. Robert Kagan, *Of Paradise and Power: America and Europe in the New World Order* (New York: Knopf, 2003), p. 33.

30. Keith Banting, George Hoberg and Richard Simeon, *Degrees of Freedom: Canada and the United States in a Changing World* (Montreal: McGill-Queen, 1997), p. 400.

31. Environics, 2000.

32. Mathew Mendelson, Centre for Research and Information, July 2002, results of a public opinion survey conducted in July and October 2002, and presented at the Borderlines Conference, Montreal, Institute for Research on Public Policy (IRPP), October 2002.

33  Policy Research Initiative, Canada–United States Comparative Data, OECD, 2000, p. 8.

34. Homeland Security Act <http://news.Findlaw.com/wp/docs/terrorism/hsa2002.pdf>

35. Lawrence Martin, *The Presidents and the Prime Ministers: Washington and Ottawa Face to Face, The Myth of Bilateral Bliss, 1867–1982* (Toronto: Doubleday Canada, 1983), p. 21.

## Chapter 6

1. Michael Bliss, "The End of English Canada," *National Post*, January 15, 2003.

2. Harry Arthurs, "Globalization of the Mind: Canadian Elites and the Restructuring of Legal Fields," *Canadian Journal of Law and Society* 12, no. 2 (February 1997).

3. John Ruggie, "Territoriality and beyond: Problematizing modernity in international relations," *International Organization* 47, no. 1 (Winter 1993), p. 157.

4. Arthurs, "Globalization of the Mind" p. 228–29.

5. Sheema Khan, "Deliver Us from Suspicion," *Globe and Mail,* November 24, 2003.

6. Marina Jimenez, "Arrested Pakistanis make refugee claims," *Globe and Mail,* September 19, 2003.

7. For a review of the legal implications of Bill C-11, "An Act respecting immigration to Canada and the granting of refugee protection to persons who are displaced, persecuted or in danger," see Audrey

Macklin, "Borderline Security," Public Law and Legal Theory Research Paper no. 02-03, University of Toronto Law School. <http://papers.ssrn.com/abstract=294321>

8. Barbara Jackman, immigration lawyer, CBC, June 26, 2003.
9. Campbell Clark, "Auditor General alarm sounded on border control: Auditor General questions screening of immigrants, rates of deportation," *Globe and Mail*, April 9, 2003.
10. David Marr and Marian Wilkinson, *Dark Victory* (Sydney: Allen & Unwin, 2003).
11 The report is found at <www.usdoj.gov/oig/igspecr1.htm>, April 29, 2003.
12. Gore Vidal, *Perpetual War for Perpetual Peace: How We Got to be So Hated* (New York: Thunder's Mouth Press, 2002).
13. T. Alexander Aleinikoff and Douglas Klusmeyer, *Citizenship Policies for an Age of Migration* (Washington, D.C.: Carnegie Endowment for International Peace, 2002), p. 64 and 88.
14. Ibid., p. 67.

## Epilogue

1. Sena Jeter Naslund, *Ahab's Wife*, (New York: Harper Collins, 1999), p. 197. In *Killshot* (Mass Market Paperback, 2003), Elmore Leonard begins his novel in Toronto's own Silver Dollar bar of the Waverly Hotel on Spadina Avenue, but it is not about Toronto at all. The hero picks up and leaves for Detroit by the end of page one. Toronto is little more than background for his larger story.
2. Theodore Levitt, "The Globalization of Markets," *Harvard Business Review* (May-June 1983).
3. Recall also rival competing symbols that invoke the asymmetry of power, particular the American icons of the flag and the border. These States-centric emblems are exclusive, nationalistic icons affirming the power of the US.
4. S.D. Clark, quoted in Seymour Martin Lipsett, *Continental Divide: The Values and Institutions of the United States and Canada* (London: Routledge, 1989), p. 51.

# A NOTE ON SOURCES

The single best visual source on the border remains the film "Between Friends/Entre Amis," produced by the National Film Board in 1976. Another essential source is Norman Nicholson's *The Boundaries of Canadian Federalism*, published in 1979, which is indispensable on the early boundaries and the mapping of Canada and North America. Francis M. Carroll's *A Good and Wise Measure: The Search for the Canadian-American Boundary, 1783–1842* (2001), contains important background material. It can be profitably supplemented by Derek Hayes' *Historical Atlas of Canada: Canada's History Illustrated with Original Maps* (2002), thanks to which the reader can see how the dots on the map were joined together from the colonial to modern eras. The distinguished economic geographer D.W. Meinig's three-volume study, *The Shaping of America* (1986), is indispensable for an understanding of the forces shaping North America from earliest times to the present. It is compelling, brilliant and a rich mine of materials. It deserves a wider public.

Seymour Martin Lipset's *Continental Divide: The Values and Institutions of the United States and Canada* (1991) is one of the classic comparisons of the institutions, values and practices of the two North American giants. *Staples, Markets and Cultural Change: Selected Essays of Harold Innis*, edited by Daniel Drache (1995), contains some of the most powerful analyses of Canada–United States relations from a staples, centre-periphery perspective. Michael Adams *Fire and Ice* (2003) is the current definitive word on Canadian values in a North American context. Another invaluable study of the Canada-US relationship examining the "mythic buzz" between the chief executives of the two countries is Lawrence Martin, *The Presidents and the Prime Ministers, Washington and Ottawa Face to Face: The Myth of Bilateral Bliss,*

*1867–1982* (1983).The two classic statements of the "end of Canada" are George Grant's *Lament for a Nation: The Defeat of Canadian Nationalism* (1965), and Thomas Courchene and Colin R. Telmer's *From Heartland to North American Region-State: The Social, Fiscal and Federal Evolution of Ontario* (1998). Richard Gwyn, *The 49th Paradox: Canada in North America* (Toronto: McClelland and Stewart, 1985) makes the compelling case that the chronic weakness of English Canadian nationalism has not been an effective counterweight to North American integration.

Other indispensable general works include John Torpey's *The Invention of the Passport: Surveillance, Citizenship and the State* (2000). Henry Nash Smith's *Virgin Land: The American West as Symbol and Myth* (1970) is a classic account of power, territory and American self-interest. Thomas Wilson and Hastings Donnan's *Border Identities: Nation and State at International Frontiers* (1998) provides a critical comparative analysis of frontiers and borders. John Wirth's essay, "Advancing the North American Community" in *Identities in North America: The Search for Community*, edited by Robert L. Earle and John D. Wirth (1995), is the most powerfully argued case for deepening the North American community and explains the obstacles in the way of this project. Stephen Clarkson's *Uncle Sam and Us* (2003) takes the opposite viewpoint on NAFTA. For those with an historical interest in the North American perspective, John Herd Thompson and Stephen Randall's *Canada and the United States: Ambivalent Allies* (1997) is indispensable.

The literature on US foreign policy post-9/11 is voluminous. Among some of the most stimulating analyses of US national interests are: Benjamin Barber's *Fear's Empire: War, Terrorism and Democracy* (2003) and Clyde Prestowitz's *Rogue Nation: The Failure of Good Intentions* (2003). Other important contributions include Robert Kagan's *Of Paradise and Power: America and Europe in the New World Order* (2003). The important question of sovereignty is examined by Stephen D. Krasner in *Problematic Sovereignty: Contested Rules and Political Possibilities* (2001). On the end of the US welfare state, see R. Kent Weaver, *Ending Welfare As We Know It* (2000), which provides an authoritative examination of a complex policy area. Paul Krugman's highly stylized *Geography and Trade* (1991) is a minor classic, challenging many myths about the dynamics of North American development.

On the economics of colony and empire in American history, see William Robbins' *Colony and Empire: The Capitalist Transformation of the American West* (1995). A postmodern treatment of the frontier is powerfully developed in Kerwin Lee Klein's *Frontiers of Historical Imagination: Narrating the European Conquest of North America, 1890–1990* (1997). Allan Moorehead's *The White Nile* (1960) remains a great classic of empire and the partition of Africa by colonial powers. Margaret MacMillan's *Paris 1919: Six Months That Changed the World* (2002) is one of the most insightful accounts of the way war and great-power diplomacy changed the map of the world with the Treaty of Versailles. Robert Sidelsky's *John Maynard Keynes: Fighting for Britain, 1937–1946* (2001) raises the curtain on Washington's special relationship with Britain and offers much food for thought about whether friendship is a strategic category of international relations and, if so, under what conditions. Sidelsky soberly concludes that despite Britain's enormous sacrifices in World War II and the brilliance of Keynes, he did not succeed in negotiating a post-war loan from Washington on terms helpful to Britain.

A wealth of information on convergence and divergence in the area of public policy is found in a book edited by Keith Banting, George Hoburg and Richard Simeon, *Degrees of Freedom: Canada and the United States in a Changing World* (1997). A subsequent volume edited by G. Hobert *Capacity for Choice: Canada in a New North America* (2002) brings the story up to date. Andrew Cohen's *While We Slept: How We Lost Our Place in the World* (2003) examines Canada's declining role and status globally. John Ralston Saul's popularly written and provocative *Reflections of a Siamese Twin: Canada at the End of the Twentieth Century* (1987) explores the important similarities and sharp differences between the two superficially look-alike societies. Robert Babcock of the University of Maine publishes the invaluable periodical *Canadian-American Public Policy,* which tracks and analyzes Canada-US policy on a wide range of issues.

On the economic effects of integration, the literature is massive. I have made only a few suggestions. For comparative purposes, the special issue of the *Journal of Economic Perspec-*

*tives*, edited by Brad de Jong (15, no.1, Winter 2000) is one of the best. John Helliwell's *How Much Do National Borders Matter?* and his subsequent monograph, *Globalization and Well-being* (2003) are pioneering studies about the interface between social policy and trade. The *Canada Watch Special Issue: Canada-US Relations in the New Millennium* (8, no.4/5, November/December 2002) is available at www.robarts.yorku.ca. For a review of NAFTA effects and much of the literature, see Daniel Drache, "Happy Fifth Birthday, NAFTA: Thinking Outside the Box" at the same website.

# ACKNOWLEDGMENTS

This book has received much help and encouragement from diverse quarters. Early on, Seth Feldman, Distinguished Robarts Chair 2000, provided materials and ideas on Turner's frontier thesis. He has been a constant critic and a wellspring of ideas. Harry Arthurs gave the manuscript a close, critical read that challenged many of its assumptions, and his feedback made a crucially important difference. Michael Adams has been a persistent and supportive critic of this extended reflection and gave generously of his time. Stephen Flynn, Jim Rosenau, George Haynal and Keith Banting have been very helpful in different ways by making materials available to me.

Susan Bradley and Daniel Turbeville made important suggestions about the US side of the border. Isidro Morales was helpful and encouraging. Other early readers included Roberto Perin and Stephen Clarkson. As always, Duncan Cameron was particularly encouraging and helpful in finding new material for the latter stages of the book. Particular thanks to Ken Coates and John M. Findlay for sharing their unpublished chapter on border crossings along the Canada-US frontier and their scholarship on the Canadian-US West. Art Davis reminded me of George Grant's essay "In Defence of North America." The talented Bruce Little of the *Globe and Mail* answered many of my queries about Statistics Canada data, and I have used some of his empirical benchmarking material. Donna Dasko graciously helped brainstorm the title. From Australia, Ian Marsh and Warwick Wilson were also helpful and supportive. Victor Lopez Villefane, ITESM, Monterrey, Mexico, offered good feedback.

Closer to home, Marlene Shore, Rob Vipond and David DeWitt provided important feedback. Special thanks in particular to Carol Wise for her many wise and detailed suggestions and her particularly sharp pencil. Dick Stanley invited me to give a seminar to Heritage Canada on citizenship and the border in January 2003. Having to present my argument cogently for non-experts forced me to rework much of the material and refocus the manuscript. Thus, Dick is indirectly responsible for the way the book turned out. Andy Cooper, Louis Pauly, Engin Isin, Richard Simeon and Gerry Boychuk were very helpful during the later stages of my work. Marjorie Cohen helped with her critical reading of the manuscript. Dr. J. Trachtenberg and Dr. H. Ipp provided critical medical support and deserve particular mention. Rob Lawrie added much with his contrarian advice and strong support. John Fraser, Master of Massey College, made finishing the manuscript much easier while I was a Senior Resident during my sabbatical year.

All of our Lake Vernon friends—John Melton, Rick Keevil, John and Jan Pierce, Jim and Gail Brown and Len Clarke and family—helped in more ways than they realized.

Marc Froese has been particularly splendid and generous in the preparation and editing of the manuscript. Special thanks for his interest throughout and in helping to prepare the two figures and many other suggestions. His feedback made a difference in the final manuscript. Laura Taman played a large and important role in the editorial process at different stages and through the many drafts that she read with good humour. Her assistance made a critical difference throughout. For their editorial excellence and patience individually and collectively, the Fernwood team of Douglas Beall, Brenda Conroy, Richard Slye, Errol Sharpe and Beverley Rach deserve special thanks for going the extra distance.

A very early version of this book was presented at the "Fourth International Congress of the Americas" at UDLA, Puebla, Mexico, in September 1999 and at "Rethinking the Line: The Canada-US Border" in Vancouver during October 2000, at a conference organized by the Policy Research Secretariat, Government of Canada. Subsequently its focus and emphasis were reoriented in a very different direction. Other dress rehearsals were presented at the Robarts Centre Summer Institute, "The Americas after the Quebec Summit: Hemispheric Integration and Social Cohesion, Civil Society and Building the New Agenda" in July 2001; at the Russian Association of Canadian Studies of St. Petersburg Bi-

Annual Meeting in June 2001; at ITESM, in Monterrey, Mexico, November 2002; and at Harvard in May 2003 at the Weatherhead Center, "On the Edge: Is the Canadian Model Sustainable?"

No one can write about the Canada-US border without seeing its direct effects on friends and associates. Norman Feltes (1932–2000) was a Canadian by choice and an American by birth, a gifted academic, former war resister, ex-marine, social justice activist, Canadian patriot, Innis scholar and friend whose own writing on border effects served, in part, as an inspiration for the way identities can co-exist. Howard Buchbinder (1927–2004) also came to Canada over thirty years ago and enriched it by his presence. As a social worker, academic, radical activist and good friend over the years, he also made a critical difference to many of my ideas. His interest in the border made a difference in the manner in which this book has evolved, and his life embodied many of the complexities of the North American reality.

Most importantly, Charlotte Drache-Lambert and Marilyn Lambert-Drache, both born outside of Canada, had a constant presence throughout the writing and redrafting of this book and contributed much. Many special thanks to them. In our family, like many others, borders matter more than ever!

# ALSO WRITTEN OR EDITED BY DANIEL DRACHE (AND OTHERS)

*The Market or the Public Domain: Global Governance and the Asymmetry of Power,* ed. (Routledge, 2001).

*Health Reform: Public Success, Private Failure,* and Terry Sullivan, eds. (Routledge, 1999).

*States Against Markets: The Limits of Globalization,* and Robert Boyer, eds. (Routledge, 1996).

*Warm Heart, Cold Country: Fiscal and Social Policy Reform in Canada,* and Andrew Ranachan, eds. (Caledon Institute, 1995).

*Staples, Markets and Cultural Change: The Centenary Edition of Harold Innis' Collected Essays,* ed. (McGill-Queen's, 1995).

*Canada and the Global Economy* (University of Athabasca, 1994).

*The Changing Workplace: Reshaping Canada's Industrial Relations System,* and Harry Glasbeek (Lorimer, 1992).

*Getting On Track: Social Democratic Strategies for Ontario,* and John O'Grady, eds. (McGill-Queen's, 1992).

*Negotiating with a Sovereign Quebec,* and R. Perin, eds. (James Lorimer, 1992).

*The New Era of Global Competition: State Policy and Market Power,* Meric Gertler, eds. (McGill-Queen's, 1991).

*Politique et Régulation Modele de Développement et Trajectoire Canadienne* (et Gérard Boismenu) (Méridien/L'Harmattan, 1990).

# INDEX